Comedy Comes Clean

Comedy Comes Clean

A HILARIOUS COLLECTION OF WHOLESOME JOKES, QUOTES, AND ONE-LINERS

Compiled by
Adam Christing

Crown Trade Paperbacks
New York

Published by Crown Trade Paperbacks, 201 East 50th Street, New
York, New York 10022.
Member of the Crown Publishing Group.

Random House, Inc. New York, Toronto, London, Sydney, Auckland

http://www.randomhouse.com/

Crown Trade Paperbacks and colophon are trademarks of Crown
Publishers, Inc.

Printed in the United States of America

Library of Congress Cataloging-in-Publication Data is available upon
request

ISBN: 0-517-88736-3

10 9 8 7 6 5 4 3 2 1

First Edition

*To my dear wife, Lisa,
with much love and gratitude*

Acknowledgments

Thanks to:

My entire family, especially my wife Lisa, our kids Leanna and Randy for their love and patience, my uncle Tod, and my parents Paul and Marianne Brown for creating a home where laughter was abundant.

The staff, performers, and friends of CLEAN COMEDIANS, particularly Shiloh "Rowan" Ahlstrand; Eric Baesel, who makes clients and comedians happy; Stacey Barnes, who helped me edit and compile this book; Bessie and Beulah; Bobbi Bourbonnais; Steve Bridges; Randy Budnikas; Jason and Tricia Chase; Scott Derrickson; Paula Draper; John Hakel; Bruce "Charlie" Johnson; Ray Jones; Paul McGinty; Guy Owen; Broderick Rice; Sid and Nancy Rogers; Ken Sands; Jeff and Harlene Scattareggia; Phil Snyder; Cary Trivanovich, who gave me the idea for CLEAN COMEDIANS; and Greg Wilson.

My major contributors, Nick Arnette, a wonderful comic and a super dude; Bill Jones, who faxed me jokes on the spot and got me *Into the Music*; Robert G. Lee, the country's brightest Christian comedian; Brad Stine, who never fails to be hilarious; and Scott Wood, a living gold mine of comedy. These guys are good friends and were very generous with their funny stuff.

My agent, Joel Fishman, who came to me with the idea for this book and told me I was his favorite client; and my editor, Wendy Hubbert, who saw the potential for the book and even installed a temporary comedy club at Crown Publishers, Inc.

Contents

Introduction

*Mark my words, when a society has to resort to the rest
room for its humor, the writing is on the wall.*
—Alan Bennett

A few years ago, I was watching a video with my son, my
dad, and my grandfather. My son Randy is six, I am
thirty-two, my dad is sixty, and my grandfather is eighty-
eight. Four generations together, and we were all laughing so hard we scared the cat out of the house. We were
watching Laurel and Hardy's classic comedy short *The
Music Box,* and afterward I realized what it was about
Stan and Ollie's movie that made it appeal to all four of
us. Nearly all of the great comedy from this century has
garnered big laughs without getting dirty.

That has become my personal and professional
motto. In 1990 I co-founded an entertainment company,
Clean Comedians, made up of cutting-edge contemporary comic performers. Since then, I've been over-
whelmed by the enthusiasm of people who, like you,
are breathing a sigh of relief that it may actually be safe
now to take the family to a comedy show. *Clean Comedians* perform in front of more than a million people
each year! I don't enjoy the vulgarity associated with the
entertainment industry today, and I'm clearly far from

alone. This book is living proof that it doesn't have to be filthy to be funny.

I'm convinced that the dining room is more amusing than the barroom. The kitchen creates more "killer comedy" than the nightclub, and the family room is funnier than the bathroom. So with COMEDY COMES CLEAN, I've compiled a book of *family* entertainment.

I've selected a big batch of topics that each of us deals with all the time, including sports, school, work, the media, dieting, kids, friends, and parents. You'll hear from a wide variety of more than fifty funny people: Everyday jokesters like mothers, politicians, children, celebrities, and other wise guys and gals will crack you up, along with professional comics ranging from the timeless—Bill Cosby and Bob Newhart—to the contemporary—Steven Wright and Jay Leno—to rising stars like Brad Stine and Robert G. Lee.

COMEDY COMES CLEAN is a gold mine of quotable, laugh-out-loud humor. You'll enjoy reading it from beginning to end, and you just may find yourself sprinkling a few gems into your next sales presentation. If you're a business manager, you can put your people at ease with wholesome humor. Go ahead—be the life of the party! Teachers—try using a few of these one-liners to lower the learning defenses of your students. Make 'em laugh during your next lesson, speech, staff meeting, or Sunday School discussion.

This humor had to pass a two-part test: It had to be clean *and* funny. It may be wacky, warped, and witty, but it isn't GROSS! As I have scanned through scores of humorous writings and recordings and downloaded the funny bones of my fellow entertainers, I have eliminated the Gender-bashing jokes, Racist material, Obscenity, Sexual inuendo, and Swearing. What's left? A hilarious collection of wholesome humor. This is a book you can give without fear to your mother-in-law, your secretary, your son, your teacher. It's so funny, it'll crack you up even if clean doesn't happen to be your thing.

I've done my best to attribute each entry to its original creator, and in the case of "old standards," I have credited the joke to the individuals whose names have become associated with the material in recent years. I hope you'll be as tickled by these jokes as I am, and if you send me your favorite clean and funny joke, side-splitting story, or quirky quote (see the back of this book for more information), I'd love to consider your comical contribution for a future volume of COMEDY COMES CLEAN.

Every area of your life is a gigantic source of humor and fun, so give yourself the gift of laughter. Enjoy !

Comedy Comes Clean

Days Like These

I have no respect for gangs today. None. They just drive by and shoot people. At least in the old days, like in West Side Story, the gangs used to dance with each other first.
—Robert G. Lee

These are strange days indeed. Sometimes you've got to laugh so you don't cry. I learned this at a very young age. One day in fourth grade, the biggest kid in school wanted to fight me. As he clenched his fist, I realized that I couldn't possibly beat him up.

So I tried to crack him up instead. I started making him laugh as he chased me around the school yard. Before long, he forgot what he was so upset about and we became friends.

Humor helps us cope with the craziness around us. The truth is often stranger than fiction, and it's a whole lot funnier. Guess who said this: "The day you take complete responsibility for yourself—the day you stop making any excuses, that's the day you start at the top." Yep—O.J. Simpson. Really. (There, we got it over with. You knew there had to be at least one O.J. line somewhere along the way.)

You may not be able to avoid all the madness in the world. But with the help of these outrageous observations, you can always choose to be amused!

• • •

That's Life . . .

I feel like I'm in a rut. Every time I go to bed at night, I find myself just getting up again in the morning.
—*Brad Stine*

I just recently had my Visa card stolen. . . . Right now it's everywhere I want to be.
—*Scott Wood*

Doesn't it bother you when people litter? The most creative rationale for throwing an apple core out the window is "It will plant seeds for other trees to grow." And of course, our highways are lined with apple trees—right next to the cigarette bush.
—*Nick Arnette*

We should have a way of telling people they have bad breath without hurting their feelings. "Well, I'm bored. . . . Let's go brush our teeth." Or, "I've got to make a phone call, hold this gum in your mouth."
—*Brad Stine*

Times have sure changed. Yesterday a bum asked me if I could spare $2.75 for a double cappuccino with no foam.
—*Bill Jones*

Strange Changes

I called the Psychic Friends Network. They said, "Who's calling?" I said, "You tell me."
—*Broderick Rice*

I live in Los Angeles. It's kind of scary. What do I do as a parent if someday my son wants to join a gang? Do I car-pool drive-by shootings?
—*Robert G. Lee*

I never expected to see the day when girls would get sunburned in the places they now do.
—*Will Rogers*

I bought an irregular electric blanket. . . .
It's solar powered.
—*Nick Arnette*

Everything is going to be automated in the future. Even Emergency 911: "Thank you for calling Emergency 911. If you're being murdered, press 1. If you're suffering from a split personality, press 2, 3, and 4. If you're battling Satan, press 666. If you are being assaulted, press pound, pound, pound. If you are already dead, stay on the line, and an operator will be with you shortly."
—*Adam Christing*

There was an item in the paper today. A lion got loose
in the Central Park Zoo. And was severely mauled.
—*Bob Newhart*

I saw a bumper sticker on a Mercedes that said,
"I brake for tax shelters."
—*Nick Arnette*

There cannot be a crisis next week.
My schedule is already full.
—*Henry Kissinger*

Now in L.A. we hope for an earthquake or a flood.
It would be nice to go through a trial outside of the
courtroom.
—*Adam Christing*

I remember when people used to step outside a moment for a breath of fresh air. Now sometimes you have
to step outside for days before you get it.
—*Victor Borge*

When I put on my acid-washed jeans,
I started having flashbacks.
—*Nick Arnette*

I hate waking up every morning to my alarm. I always
bang my head on the steering wheel.
—*Scott Wood*

Forward March

You can't say civilization isn't advancing; in every war
they kill you in a new way.
—*Will Rogers*

Some people's idea of "roughing it" is not having cable.
—*Nick Arnette*

Cordless phones are great. If you can find them.
—*Glenn Foster*

I grew up in a neighborhood so rough, I learned to
read by the light of a police helicopter.
—*Bill Jones*

Countries are making nuclear weapons
like there's no tomorrow.
—*Emo Philips*

These days, there's "virtual reality," "virtual shopping,"
and "virtual banking," all done by computer. I'm way
ahead of everybody. I've been getting a "virtual pay-
check" for years.
—*Bill Jones*

Swiss Army Knives got their names because it takes the entire Swiss army just to carry one.
—*Nick Arnette*

Minor Adjustments

I passed a car dealership. I looked in the window and I saw the most beautiful cars. And a fellow came out and said, "Come on in, they're bigger than ever and they last a lifetime!" He was talking about the payments.
—*Corbett Monica*

When people ask me if I have any spare change, I tell them I have it at home in my spare wallet.
—*Nick Arnette*

The cost of living is going up and the chance of living is going down.
—*Flip Wilson*

Banks charge a "service fee" to use an ATM. Coke machines will soon expect a tip!
—*Bill Jones*

I had my car stereo ripped off last week. The police said it looked like a professional did it. I said, "What did he do, leave a business card, DASHBOARD REDESIGNED BY ROCCO!"

—*Nick Arnette*

My neighborhood is so dangerous, America On Line won't even deliver E-mail here.
—*Bill Jones*

My father invented the burglar alarm—which unfortunately was stolen from him.
—*Victor Borge*

Travelin' Light

I travel everywhere I go, otherwise
I wouldn't get anywhere.
—Brad Stine

As an entertainer, I travel a lot. I once saw a pin on a Delta Airlines employee and I asked him what the letters in "Delta" stand for. He said, "Don't Expect Luggage To Arrive."

With or without suitcases in hand, it seems like all of us are constantly on the move. And even with high-speed automobiles, overnight delivery, and jet travel, we all want things to go even faster. My friend Mike Horton once caught himself yelling at the fax machine to hurry up!

We need to cheer up more than we need to hurry up. Whether you are taking a cruise, flying on a business trip, or dealing with the extreme heat or cold of an exotic new locale, this globe-trotting humor will help you enjoy the ride.

• • •

Cruising Along

What a lucky thing the wheel was invented before the automobile; otherwise, can you imagine what awful screeching?

—*Samuel Hoffenstein*

I just rolled into town . . . because I was driving a Suzuki Samurai.

—*Nick Arnette*

I love those signs along the highway that say, "Litter Removal Next 2 Miles." That's when I start chucking my trash out the window.

—*Scott Wood*

My wife and I went on a three-day cruise. Actually, it was more like a three-day meal. They tell you to bring just one outfit, but in three different sizes: large, extra large, and blimp.

—*Robert G. Lee*

We've all heard the stat that it's safer to fly in a plane than to drive in a car. What about the stat that says it's safer to *crash* in a car than it is in a plane?! You get in a car wreck, people say, "Was anyone hurt?" You get in a plane wreck, people say, "Was anyone *recognizable?*"

—*Brad Stine*

Camping isn't what it used to be. "Honey, I'm gonna go get some firewood, do you have change for a twenty?"
—*Nick Arnette*

Anybody in the audience with a New York license plate BL75836745895947362847456578392610284, will you kindly move it. Your license plate is blocking traffic.
—*Bill Dana*

We went on the cruise for romance, but my wife and I found that by the time we got back to the cabin we were so stuffed, we were in pain, "Ow, don't touch me. I can't move. I want to die. What time is it? Midnight buffet? Let's go!"
—*Robert G. Lee*

Q: What kind of car does a dude drive?
A: Dude-A-Baker.
—*Nick Arnette*

Whenever I travel by plane someone *always* says, "Have a safe trip." Since when does a safe plane flight become my responsibility? I'm not even sure what I'm supposed to do! Go kick the tires, drug test the pilot, what? I feel I'm doing my part by not going up to the cockpit every five minutes and asking, "Are we there yet?"
—*Brad Stine*

Air Lines

After the flight attendants tell about all the safety features, I always play a trick on them. I bring little catsup packets and pour one just below each ear. Then I call the stewardess over, point to my ears and ask, "Is *this* supposed to happen?"

—*Brad Stine*

Two men jump from an airplane. The first pulls the cord—and the chute works perfectly. The second pulls the cord—and nothing happens. He keeps falling straight down.

As he passes his friend, the guy gets mad, unbuckles the harness, and shouts, "So, you wanna race, eh?"

—*Charlie Callas*

A collision occurs when two motorists go after the same pedestrian.

—*H. Alan Dunn*

Airplanes are the ultimate in consolidation. Flight attendants instruct us, "We have a flotation device, but actually, it's your seat!" I'm paranoid to throw anything away, I might need it later. For all I know, my empty peanut bag is my life raft.

—*Brad Stine*

I think airline flights should be cheaper. At the airport, they always make you walk at least halfway to your destination before you even get on the plane.

—*Nick Arnette*

The scientific theory I like best is that the rings of Saturn are composed entirely of lost airline luggage.

—*Mark Russell*

I must admit I'm selfish. It's not something I'm proud of, but I think everybody's like me to a certain extent. For example, if there's a plane crash, there are four basic questions I ask:

1. Was I on it?
2. Was anybody I love on it?
3. Was anybody who owed me money on it?
And finally,
4. Will my flight be delayed because of it?

If the answer to all four is no, then I'm sorry, but I've got to move on.

—*Robert G. Lee*

I got a wonderful tribute at the airport. They fired twenty-one shots in the air in my honor. Of course, it would've been nicer if they'd waited for the plane to land.

—*Bob Hope*

The way the new jets go, you can have dinner on one
continent and heartburn on the next.
—*The Humor Gazette*

Unexpected Arrivals

I just bought a new car. I asked for the passenger side
air bag. They gave me the salesman.
—*Nick Arnette*

When you look like your passport photo,
it's time to go home.
—*Erma Bombeck*

Q: What do you call a dude from Iceland?
A: Cool Dude.
—*Nick Arnette*

We were coming back into New York Harbor and we
went under the Verrazano Bridge and I got a lump in my
throat. We went under the Brooklyn Bridge and I started
to cry . . . because we *flew* home.
—*Totie Fields*

Of course, America had often been discovered before Columbus, but it had always been hushed up.
—*Oscar Wilde*

Q: What do you call a dude from Mexico?
A: Medudo.
—*Nick Arnette*

I have just returned from Boston. It is the only thing to do if you find yourself there.
—*Fred Allen*

What a hotel we're staying at! The towels are so big and fluffy, you can hardly close your suitcase.
—*Bessie and Beulah*

I just went to Las Vegas in July. Because I am the stupidest man in the world.

People live there—on purpose. What would make anyone start a town that gets to 128 degrees? "Well, we don't have enough fuel to make it to the surface of the *sun*; let's live here."
—*Brad Stine*

Las Vegas. It's a Mexican word. It means "Move."
—*Brad Stine*

Marriage Mirth

Keep your eyes wide open before marriage,
and half-shut afterwards.
—Benjamin Franklin

Love is blind. Marriage is an institution. Does this mean that marriage is an institution for the blind?

Marriage has been a target for humorists throughout the ages. It's been called a three-ring circus: the engagement *ring,* the wedding *ring,* the suffe*ring.* If you are single, you may read this chapter and feel confident that you are smarter than your married friends.

This chapter contains the musings of comics like Scott Wood and Robert G. Lee, who make their living making jokes about marriage, side-by-side with the comments of actress Zsa Zsa Gabor, who made a career making marriages into a joke.

I think marriage is a really good thing. And humor is one of the keys to enjoying a lifetime together. Remember, when things get difficult, if you can laugh together, you can live together.

* * *

′ My wife thinks I'm too nosy. At least that's what she keeps scribbling in her diary.
—*Drake Sather*

A man in love is incomplete until he has married.
Then he's finished.
—*Zsa Zsa Gabor*

A lot of people wonder how you know if you're really in love. Just ask yourself this one question: "Would I mind being destroyed financially by this person?"
—*Ronnie Shakes*

The sure way to tell if a man is a bachelor is to check his silverware. If it's full of nicks from going through the garbage disposal a couple of dozen times, he's for real.
—*Nick Arnette*

Explain weddings to me. A bride will make her best friends in the whole world wear the ugliest dresses known to mankind. And she will lie to them by saying, "I'm sure you can wear it again!" To which every bridesmaid is thinking, Sure I will, if the Polka Festival ever comes to town.
—*Robert G. Lee*

I'm having trouble managing the mansion.
What I need is a wife.
—*Ella Tambussi Grasso (first woman
to be a U.S. governor)*

I'm thinking about getting married. I looked up the word "engaged" in the dictionary. It said, "To do battle with the enemy." Then I looked up mother-in-law. It said, "See engaged."

—Scott Wood

Before marriage, a man will lie awake all night thinking about something you said; after marriage, he'll fall asleep before you finish saying it.

—Helen Rowland

The only time a woman really succeeds in changing a man is when he's a baby.

—Natalie Wood

I'd like to go to an assertiveness training class. First I need to check with my wife.

—Adam Christing

When an admiring lady fan wrote to ask Richard Brinsley Sheridan the essential difference between man and woman, the famous British playwright replied:

```
Dear Madam,

I cannot conceive.

Sincerely yours,

Richard Brinsley Sheridan
```

—Dear Wit

A very attractive realtor looked across the table at her husband, who seemed to be gaining weight by the hour. She said, "Honey, if you don't stop adding-on and start remodeling, "I'm going to trade up."
—*Bill Jones*

When a couple of young people, strongly devoted to each other, commence to eat onions, it is safe to pronounce them engaged.
—*James Bailey*

My first wife divorced me on grounds of incompatibility, and besides, I think she hated me.
—*Oscar Levant*

A woman was out driving with her husband. She was speeding along about fifty. Suddenly a motorcycle cop appeared alongside and told her to pull over. The cop looked at her. "Hmmm!" he said. "I'm going to put you down for fifty-five." She turned to her husband. "See! I told you this hat makes me look old."
—*Joe Laurie, Jr.*

She's going to make some man a good wife someday, provided he comes down off the movie screen and asks her.
—*Thorton Wilder*

HUSBAND: "Darling, will you love me when I'm old and
feeble?"
WIFE: "Of course I do."
                    —*H. Alan Dunn*

A primer for any couple should be the book *Men Are
from Mars, Women Are from Venus.* It explains that men
and women are from different planets. For example, women like to verbalize their feelings on relation-
ships. It's difficult for a man to even admit he's in a
relationship.
                    —*Robert G. Lee*

I know a couple that got remarried. He missed two
alimony payments and she repossessed him.
                    —*Bill Barner*

'Tis more blessed to give than to receive;
for example, wedding presents.
                    —*H. L. Mencken*

My girlfriend and I are talking about getting married.
She keeps asking me if I can support her, but she knows
I can; she's always on my back.
                    —*Scott Wood*

After fifteen years of marriage, my wife wants us to
recommit our vows. As a man, I don't understand her

need to get married again. We've got our toaster, let's move on!

—*Robert G. Lee*

I was the best man at the wedding. So why is she marrying *him?*

—*Jerry Seinfeld*

A Harvard University boy got his old father in Maine to come to Cambridge and see the football game between Yale and Harvard. As they sat down, the boy slapped his father on the back and said, "Dad, for three dollars you are going to see more fight, more life, and more enthusiasm than you ever saw before." The old man smiled and replied, "I am not so sure about that, Son. That's what I paid for my marriage license."

—*Rev. James Whitcomb Brougher, Sr.*

Beulah just had plastic surgery. Her husband cut up her credit cards.

—*Bessie and Beulah*

I think—therefore I'm single.

—*Lizz Winstead*

If I ever got divorced, on the singles scene, I'd be worth about as much as an eight-track at a garage sale.

—*Robert G. Lee*

When a man makes a woman his wife, it's the highest compliment he can pay her, and it's usually the last.
—Helen Rowland

I've been married to the same woman for fourteen years. Which is like eighty-something in L.A. years.
—Robert G. Lee

High heels were invented by a woman who had been kissed on the forehead.
—Christopher Morley

When a woman takes a man for better or for worse, she may find him much worse than she took him for.
—H. Alan Dunn

I made my first million, and I owe it all to the little woman. She was two inches high. I sold her to a circus and made a million dollars.
—Dave Ketchum

If there's a girl around your office who wants the room extremely warm, you can deal with it by bringing in a man who wants it overly cold. They will marry and set up a home of their own.
—The Humor Gazette

I met my husband at a travel agency. He was looking
for a vacation and I was the last resort.
—*Bessie and Beulah*

I am a marvelous housekeeper. Every time I leave a
man I keep his house.
—*Zsa Zsa Gabor*

My husband forgot my birthday and my anniversary. I
didn't feel bad. On the contrary. Give me a guilty husband any day. Some of my best outfits come from
his guilt!
—*Betty Walker*

For a man, getting dressed up is anything that requires
underwear and socks. Whereas a woman gets her hair
done, puts on makeup, tummy toner, a short skirt, and
high heels, then says she wants to "find a man who loves
me for *me!*"
—*Robert G. Lee*

A man has arrived when he can be as cranky at the office as he is at the breakfast table.
—*The Humor Gazette*

You know your marriage is in trouble when you see
your wife on *Love Connection*.
—*Scott Wood*

Laughing from Head to Toe

His toupee makes him look twenty years sillier.
—Bill Dana

Be honest. We are all obsessed with our appearance. Admit it: Who's the first person you look for in a photograph?

We are never satisfied with the way we look. We pluck our eyebrows, enlarge our muscles, pierce our ears (and just about everything else), and tattoo various parts. And we still don't like what we see! As Phyllis Diller confessed, "When I go to the beauty parlor, I always use the emergency entrance. Sometimes I just go for an estimate."

Put that mirror down. You are about to laugh from head to toe with hysterical words of wit about the human body, from the ultimate body language story to wise guy Pete McLeod's take on the classical good news/bad news joke.

• • •

Joggers are a cocky crew. They jog with their heads held high. Jim Fixx, the guy who wrote the book on jogging, died of a heart attack while jogging. When I see joggers go by, I shout, "Jim Fixx is dead. Fats Domino lives!"
—*Jason Chase*

The only thing that can stop hair falling is the floor.
—*Will Rogers*

Our doctor is an eye, ear, nose, throat,
and wallet specialist.
—*Bessie and Beulah*

Her features did not seem to know
the value of teamwork.
—*George Ade*

I want to know what sadist decreed that we should shave certain parts of our bodies. What other animal on earth shaves? The poodle. You know how dumb they look; we are emulating a rat-dog with a bad perm.
—*Robert G. Lee*

I think it was Einstein who said, "The more I look at the universe, the more I look at myself," and the more I look at myself, the more I realize . . . I could use a comb! What was the deal on his wacky hair?! Here's a man who could contemplate relativity in his mind, yet the thought of using a brush was too complex!
—*Brad Stine*

She laughs at everything you say. Why?
Because she has fine teeth.
—*Benjamin Franklin*

I was dating this one girl who was really stupid. I once saw her in the supermarket reading the back of a shampoo bottle. . . .

"*Wet hair, lather, rinse, repeat.*
Wet hair, lather, rinse, repeat.
Wet hair, lather, rinse, repeat."
—Scott Wood

He must have had a magnificent build before his stomach went in for a career of its own.
—Margaret Halsey

How come people who are always late wear it like a badge of honor? They'll brag about it: "I'm always running late."

How can you be "running late"? If you were running, you should have made it! If you're running, you're doing it quickly! Which means some people want to be late *as fast as they can*!
—Brad Stine

My brother is really lazy. His idea of exercise is doing pull-ups on the salad bar.
—Scott Wood

You go to the ballet and you see girls dancing on their tiptoes. Why don't they just get taller girls?
—Greg Ray

I knew I was being watched. I don't know much about body language, but when I turned my head, she was giving me the eye. It was written all over her face. She played with her hair, crinkled her nose, tugged her ear, and raised her brow. It was obvious she liked me a lot—or she just had a severe nervous condition.

She was all smiles and I was all ears. My heart was racing, my palms were sweaty, and my face was flushed. It wasn't a thyroid problem; I was just head over heels.

Before I knew it, we were on the dance floor—footloose and fancy-free. You know, arm in arm, hand in hand, cheek to cheek. Thinking I swept her off her feet, I soon discovered I was just putty in her hands.

But there was more than meets the eye. There was her boyfriend. He was giving me the evil eye. In fact, if looks could kill, I'd be body-bagged and toe-tagged.

Fortunately, it was her *ex*-boyfriend. Unfortunately, he wasn't aware of that fact. He was a brain-dead knucklehead with a thick skull and a low brow. You know, in one ear and out the other.

At first, I thought he was pulling my leg, but he was serious as a heart attack. He was in my face—shaking his fist, pointing his finger, and running off at the mouth. What nerve.

He was armed to the teeth, with a hot head, a heavy hand, and a chip on his shoulder. I had an open mind, but he had a closed fist. I wanted to smooth out the wrinkles. He wanted a pound of flesh.

Half of me was wishing that this blue-eyed doll-face would've just put her nose in the air and given me the cold shoulder. But I couldn't back out now and let her slip between my fingers. So risking life and limb, I looked him straight in the eye and said, "Put your money where your mouth is, pal, or heads are gonna roll."

And just then, I thought—who the heck am I kidding? Even on my tiptoes, this guy is head and shoulders above me. I'm only knee-high to a grasshopper.

Besides, when it comes to fighting tooth and nail, I'm all thumbs and wet behind the ears. I've got two left feet, white knuckles, a yellow belly, and thin skin.

I was in over my head, knee-deep with no leg to stand on. But I couldn't just knuckle under, get cold feet, and throw my hands in the air. It was time to go face-to-face, head-to-head, and toe-to-toe. So, to get a leg up, I puffed my chest, put up my dukes, and threw my weight around.

Much to my chagrin, he just slapped his knee, split a gut, and laughed his head off. I knew I was out on a limb with one foot in the grave.

So to try and save face, I turned the other cheek, crossed my fingers, greased his palm, and begged for a change of heart. Unfortunately, my plea fell on deaf ears. That's when I knew it was time to rack my brain for a new plan.

I stood up, put my foot down, and landed a lucky sucker punch . . . right on the kisser. And it must've been his Achilles' heel, because he fell to my feet like a bag of bones . . . belly up!

At first, I thought my left hand didn't know what my right hand was doing. But when I opened my eyes, she was standing over his limp body with a clenched fist and a big smile. It was *she* that gave him a knuckle sandwich and a nose bent out of shape.

That's right, it was *a woman* that saved me by the skin of my teeth and the seat of my pants. I know it's embarrassing, but hey—it sure beats a swift kick in the . . . well, THE END.

—Greg Wilson

If all the world's a stage, shouldn't we *all* be wearing makeup?
—*Brad Stine*

He was so narrow-minded he could see through a keyhole with two eyes.
—*Esther Forbes*

I helped my nephew move yesterday. He didn't get a new home, he's just really fat!
—*Scott Wood*

Futon is a Japanese word that means "sore back."
—*Nick Arnette*

Her face was her chaperone.
—*Rupert Hughes*

My favorite word is "oops." It's a word whose only function is to say . . . it's not my fault! You trip and start to fall, "Oops." Spill something, "Oops." Don't blame *me!* Blame *gravity!* That's what "oops" stands for: gravity. That's why it's spelled O-O-P-S; it's an acronym for "Oh, our planet's spinning!"
—*Brad Stine*

Forrest Gump has taken in well over 300 million dollars. But the studio insists that it has actually lost 62 million. Maybe Forrest Gump is doing their accounting.
—*Bill Jones*

Television enables you to be entertained in your home by people you wouldn't have in your home.
—*David Frost*

VAN DAMME = Violent Action Never Decreases A Major Movie's Earnings
—*Adam Christing*

An associate producer is the only guy in Hollywood who will associate with a producer.
—*Fred Allen*

I think the movie rental place down the street is owned by the mafia. It's called Legbuster Video.
—*Scott Wood*

On cable TV, they have a weather channel—twenty-four hours of weather. We had something like that where I grew up. We called it a window.
—*Dan Spencer*

These action movie stars keep making sequels. Sylvester Stallone will soon be starring in *Blowing Up the Bridges of Madison County*. Bruce Willis will be doing yet another *Die Hard* movie, *Die Hard 4: The Rogaine Connection*.

—*Bill Jones*

There's a new *Star Wars* movie coming out. This time the evil villian is a country western singer. His name is Garth Vader.

—*Scott Wood*

New TV shows are basically old shows, reworked slightly. Here are some new shows coming your way soon:

· Bob Villa in a show about middle-aged folks having plastic surgery:
This Old Spouse.
· A whiz kid lawyer who starts a lucrative practice:
Doogie Shyster.
· Barbara Walters and Hugh Downs host a news show for older folks whose hearing and eyesight are deteriorating:
20/200.
· A miniseries on the Clinton presidency:
The Blunder Years.

—*Bill Jones*

Have you ever noticed in those old monster movies, no matter how slow the mummy walks, he always catches his victim. I saw one last night; he caught Carl Lewis.
—*Scott Wood*

Imitation is the sincerest form of television.
—*Fred Allen*

The embarrassing thing is that the salad dressing is outgrossing my films.
—*Paul Newman*

Television—a medium, so called because it is neither rare nor well done.
—*Ernie Kovacs*

Stephen King's doing a sequel to *The Lawnmower Man*. It's called *Weedwhacker Woman*.
—*Scott Wood*

On ships they call them barnacles; in radio they attach themselves to desks and are called vice presidents.
—*Fred Allen*

Did you know that Andy of Mayberry and Barney were related? They were cousins. In fact, everybody in Mayberry was related. That's how they got Goober.
—*Robert G. Lee*

It took me fifteen years to discover I had no talent for writing, but I couldn't give it up because by that time I was too famous.
—*Robert Benchley*

The price of a movie today is just too expensive. . . .
I think AMC stands for Always Making Cash.
—*Scott Wood*

A weary actor was talking to his wife about his desire to get away for a while. He whispered into her ear, "Let's run away to Maui or Tahiti . . . just your people and my people, OK?"
—*Bill Jones*

Canadians have a tough time playing *Wheel of Fortune*.
They keep saying "A" after every letter they ask for.
—*Nick Arnette*

Disney owns ABC now. There have been some changes, like:
- Peter Jennings starts the evening news saying, "Good evening . . . and here's what happened today *outside* the Happiest Place on Earth."
- Minnie Mouse is the Tool-Time Girl on *Home Improvement*.
- Superimposing mouse ears on the President during his State of the Union Address. His nose grows as he proclaims his promises!
—*Bill Jones*

I find television very educational. Every time someone turns on the set I go into the other room and read a book.

—*Groucho Marx*

They say going on TV makes you look 10 percent heavier. But watching it makes you 20 percent dumber!
—*Bill Jones*

I write for *Reader's Digest*. It's not hard. All you do is copy out an article and mail it in again.
—*Milt Kamen*

The length of a film should be directly related to the endurance of the human bladder.
—*Alfred Hitchcock*

The tabloid shows are so sleazy; my dog walks out of the room when he hears the theme to *Hard Copy.*
—*Bill Jones*

If I see one more horror movie, I'm gonna scream!
—*Scott Wood*

Employment Annoyment

Last week a friend of mind lost his job at the orange juice factory. He couldn't concentrate.

The only thing more frustrating than your job is the way other people do theirs. It's always fun to have a few laughs at the boss's expense or pull down an authority figure. For example, Q: What do you call a lawyer with an IQ of 50? A: Your Honor!

There's always something to gripe about when it comes to employment: annoying bosses, dead-end jobs, or being out of a job. I knew I was taking too many business trips away from home when my kids started calling me "Uncle."

These pages poke fun at nearly every type of work and worker. Dentists get drilled. Gas station attendants get hosed. You will also read a remarkable story of what one sailor went through just to get a few days off. But there's only one more lawyer joke!

Work will always be there to bug us, so let's have a few laughs about it.

• • •

The brain is a wonderful organ; it starts working the moment you get up in the morning and does not stop until you get into the office.

—*Robert Frost*

Realtors are people who did not make it
as used-car salesmen.
—*Bob Newhart*

What does it take to get a few days off of work?

C.O., U.S.S. *Saratoga*

Dear Captain:

When I got home I found that my father's brick silo had been struck by lightning, knocking some of the bricks off the top. I decided to fix the silo, and so I rigged up a beam, with a pulley and whip at the top of the silo, and hoisted a couple of barrels full of bricks to the top. When I got through fixing the silo there were a lot of bricks left over.

I hoisted the barrel back up again, secured the line at the bottom, and then went up and filled the barrel with the extra bricks. Then I went down to the bottom and cast off the line.

Unfortunately, the barrel of bricks was heavier than I was and before I knew what was happening, the barrel started down and jerked me off the ground. I decided to hang on, and halfway up I met the barrel coming down and received a severe blow on the shoulder. I then continued on up to the top, banging my head against the beam and getting my fingers jammed in the pulley.

When the barrel hit the ground it busted the bottom, allowing all the bricks to spill out. I was now heavier than the barrel and so started down again at high speed. Halfway down I again met the barrel and received severe injuries to my shins. When I hit the ground I landed on the bricks, getting numerous painful cuts from the sharp edges.

At this point I must have lost my presence of mind because I let go of the rope. The barrel then came down and struck me another heavy blow on the head, putting me in the hospital for three days.

Respectfully request five days extension of leave.

John Doe

—Daniel Gallery, *Clear the Decks!*

My computer is so fast. Before yours can boot up, mine has already crashed three times.
—*Bill Jones*

Living with a budget saves money because by the time you've balanced it, it's too late to go anywhere.
—*H. Alan Dunn*

They say in the future there will be no such thing as money to deal with. So I guess in that respect, things will be about the same.
—*Nick Arnette*

Dentist: A prestidigitator who, putting metal into your mouth, pulls coins out of your pocket.
—*Ambrose Bierce*

We were so poor we had to go to the bank to talk to the loan arranger. He wasn't in, so we talked to Tonto instead.
—*Bessie and Beulah*

I'm a writer. I write checks. They're not very good.
—*Wendy Liebman*

I used to work in a fire hydrant factory. You couldn't park anywhere near the place.
—*Steven Wright*

If a man keeps his trap shut, the world will beat a path to his door.
—*Franklin Adams*

I love the way everybody is getting fancy job titles. Gas station attendants are now called "petroleum consultants." They saunter over. "I'd recommend the 89 octane unleaded. It's an unpretentious little fuel with a surprising kick. Would you care to sniff the nozzle?"
—*Robert G. Lee*

Architect: One who drafts a plan of your house and plans a draft of your money.
—*Ambrose Bierce*

The gas station attendant looks at the car and says, "You got a flat tire." I said, "No, the other three just swelled up."
—*Bill Engvall*

If you want to get rich from writing, write the sort of thing that's read by persons who move their lips when they're reading to themselves.
—*Don Marquis*

He has been a doctor a year now and has had two patients—no, three, I think—yes, it was three; I attended their funerals.
—*Mark Twain*

Why is it when you pass by road construction crews on the highway nobody is working . . . except the woman who is holding the sign that says, "Slow Men Working."
—*Nick Arnette*

You have to have a physical before you get into the Army. A doctor looks in one ear, another doctor looks in the other ear, and if they can't see each other, you're in. And if they can see each other, you become an MP.
—*Joe E. Brown*

My boss at Christmas was a lot of fun: "I want you to look in your pay envelopes and you'll know that I keep the Christmas spirit around here. Because in each and every pay envelope you'll find . . . snow."

—Dave Ketchum

A bank is a place where they lend you an umbrella in fair weather and ask for it back again when it begins to rain.

—Robert Frost

Asked why she was leaving her position, a stenographer explained in her letter of resignation:

```
Dear Boss,

     My reason for quitting will soon be
apparent—and so will I.

                              Mary R.
```

—Dear Wit

Live within your income, even if you have to borrow money to do so.
—Josh Billings

The trouble with unemployment is that the minute you wake up in the morning you're on the job.
—Slappy White

No matter how much the boss likes you, if you work in a bank you can't take home samples.
—*Eddie Cantor*

I'm sure glad a realtor didn't write Abe Lincoln's life story. The tiny log cabin of his childhood would have become a "rustic country estate."
—*Bill Jones*

I got a job at Disneyland. Drove the monorail from the hotel to the park, eight hours a day, smiling. "Here we go. . . . Here we are." I did such a good job, they made me monorail supervisor. Which meant I stood on the ground and said, "There they go. . . . There they are."
—*Robert G. Lee*

WARNING TO EMPLOYEES: Firings will continue until morale improves.
—*Nameless Manager*

I used to sell life insurance. But life insurance is really strange. It's a weird concept. You really don't get anything for it. It works like this: You pay me money. And when you die, I'll pay *you* money.
—*Bill Kirchenbauer*

I'm living so far beyond my income that we may almost be said to be living apart.
—*Hector Hugh Munro*

I love my dentist. He has an X ray of his family
in the waiting room.
—*Robert G. Lee*

I know a guy who plans to make a fortune with a new
vending machine. It's a big box that says, "How gullible
are you? Insert $500."
—*Bill Jones*

If you get to thirty-five and your job still involves wearing
a name tag, you've probably made a serious vocational
error.
—*Dennis Miller*

I got a traffic ticket the other day so I went to see a
lawyer who charges by the minute. When I asked him
the first question he said, "Wwwwwwelllllllll Mmm-
mmmmissssssssssssster Aaaaaaaaaaarrrrrrrrrrrnnnnnnnnne-
eeeeete. . . ."
—*Nick Arnette*

The worst job I ever had was working in a Fotomat
booth. I was the only one at the Christmas party.
—*Mark Dobrient*

Jest Friends

He's the kind of man who picks his friends—to pieces.
—Mae West

My friend and fellow comic Jason Chase says, "You can pick your friends and you can pick your nose. But you can't pick your friend's nose."

You gotta be choosy with your friends. But you gotta have them. This chapter will give you some great jokes and a few truly funny remarks about friendship to pass along to a buddy.

Your best friends are generally those individuals you have laughed longest and hardest with. I would lay down my life for my friends. But they had better not ask me to look at their vacation pictures.

• • •

If you visit people and they give you the hide-a-bed,
you are pretty much the hide-a-friend.
—*Nick Arnette*

There are three kinds of friends: best friends, guest
friends, and pest friends.
—*Laurence J. Peter*

Three friends were stranded on a deserted island. After several weeks of no food and no drinking water, they were losing heart.

Suddenly a bottle floated onto the shore and a beautiful genie popped out. "I have three wishes to grant. Each of you gentlemen can make one wish come true."

Friend number one got excited. He said, "I wish I was in Las Vegas with dice in one hand and a drink in the other, surrounded by music, food, and beautiful women." Instantly he was gone, his wish granted.

Friend number two smiled and said, "I wish I was back home right now with my wonderful wife and our two small children, at our log cabin in the woods sitting in front of the fire and singing Christmas carols together." Just like that, he disappeared.

The genie asked the remaining man, "And what do you wish for?" He answered, "I wish I had my buddies back."

—*Tod Stoddard*

Why can we remember the tiniest detail that has happened to us, and not remember how many times we have told it to the same person?

—*François de La Rochefouauld*

He is a fine friend. He stabs you in the front.

—*Leonard Louis Levinson*

I have a friend whose life is so boring. He has a bumper sticker on his car that says, "Hit me. I need the excitement."

—*Bill Jones*

He's the kind of friend who will always be there when he needs you.
—*Adam Christing*

Mark met his old friend Steve and told him that he was in desperate need of $5,000. He begged Steve to loan it to him. Steve gave him an immediate refusal.

"I have to remind you, then," said Mark, "of what happened twenty-five years ago when we were in Vietnam together. You were lying wounded in the jungle. I crawled out to you, dodging bullets, threw you over my shoulder, and dragged you back. For this, I got the Medal of Honor. But the important thing was, I saved your life. Now, will you let me borrow the five thousand dollars?"

"No," said Steve, unimpressed.

"Let's go back to fifteen years ago," said Mark. "I'd like to remind you of who introduced you to your wife. Who set you up with her when you were afraid to ask her out? Who gave the money for your honeymoon, Steve? Me! Now, will you let me have the five thousand dollars?"

The response was again "No."

But, still determined, Mark continued. "How about ten years ago," said Mark, "when your daughter was struck by that rare disease and your doctor was desperately trying to find the right blood to give her a transfusion? Whose was it that finally matched? Your pal Mark. I gave her seven blood transfusions, and it pulled her through. You'll let me have the money, won't you, Steve?"

"No, I won't," said Steve.

"Think back to five years ago," urged Mark. "Remember when your back was against the wall and you had to have twenty-seven thousand dollars or the bank would foreclose on your company, who was it who signed the note that guaranteed your loan? Good old Mark! I saved your business for you then, didn't I, Steve? Now you will find it in your heart to loan me the five thousand dollars!"

Steve still had no problem refusing.

"What kind of friend are you, anyway?" yelled the exasperated Mark. "Twenty-five years ago I saved your life, fifteen years ago I introduced you to your wife, ten years ago I saved your daughter's life, five years ago I saved your business. In light of that, can you tell me why in the world you won't loan me the five thousand dollars?"

"What have you done for me lately?" said Steve.
—*Walter Schwimmer*

Whenever a friend succeeds, a little something
in me dies.
—*Gore Vidal*

Self-Helpings

*After twelve years of therapy, my psychiatrist
said something that brought tears to my eyes. He
said,* "No hablo ingles."
—Ronnie Shakes

More than 15 million Americans have beat addictions
by becoming hooked on recovery programs. Self-help
books are consistent best-sellers, and if you are not in a
support group, you start wondering if maybe you're hiding something. My friend asked me if I attended the
"Promise Keepers" conference. I told him, "No, I didn't
go, I *said* I was going to."

Obviously there are times when we may need to get
help from a professional counselor or therapist. But
laughter may be the best medicine of all. Here you'll
find Guy Owen's totally comprehensive recovery program, and you'll enjoy a couple of quick gems about
positive thinking. Since you've got to be hooked on
something, it might as well be humor.

• • •

There are so many twelve-step groups today:
AA = Alcoholics Anonymous. ACA = Adult Children of
Alcoholics. These are *not* inclusive enough. Here is a

recovery program that covers all the bases:

ABCDEFGHIJKLMNOPQRSTUVWXYZ = Adult Bad Children of Dysfunctional Evil Families Getting Hooked Into Just Keeping Little Mean Nasty Old People Quiet Requiring Specialized Treatment Using Valium With eXtreme unYielding Zeal.

—*Guy Owen*

I was forced to go to a positive thinking seminar. I couldn't stand it. So I went outside to the parking lot and let *half* the air out of everybody's tires. As they came out I said, "So . . . are your tires half-full or half-empty?"

—*Scott Derrickson*

Vanna White's in a rehab center. She's hooked on phonics.

—*Scott Wood*

I went to a bookstore and I asked the woman behind the counter where the self-help section was. She said, "If I told you, that would defeat the whole purpose."

—*Brian Kiley*

Ludlow Bean was arrested the other day for stealing a woman's change purse. He told the judge that he hadn't been feeling well, and he thought the change would do him good.

—*Charley Weaver*

My friend is so lazy. He paid me to go into therapy for him. He says he always hires other people to carry his baggage.

—*Bill Jones*

How many psychiatrists does it take to change a lightbulb? Only one, but the lightbulb has to really *want* to be changed.

—*Anne Eva Ricks*

How can you have a war on drugs, if drugs are an inanimate object?: "Marijuana, we know you're in that locker. Come out with your hands up!"

—*Adam Christing*

We offer sound advice. That's 99 percent sound and 1 percent advice.

—*Bessie and Beulah*

I used to be a heavy gambler. But now I just make mental bets. That's how I lost my mind.

—*Steve Allen*

My friend thought he was not gonna make it. Then he started thinking positive. Now he's positive he's not gonna make it.

—*Brother Sammy Shore*

I suffer from two phobias: (1) Phobia-phobia—the fear you're unable to get scared, and (2) Xylophataquieopi-aphobia—the fear of not pronouncing words correctly.
—*Brad Stine*

We need a twelve-step group for compulsive talkers. They could call it On Anon Anon.
—*Paula Poundstone*

He's turned his life around. He used to be depressed and miserable. Now he's miserable and depressed.
—*David Frost*

Milk Came Out My Nose!

*When you've eaten onions, don't wear a rose
in your buttonhole.*
—Bessie and Beulah

Sitting at the dinner table with my mom, dad, and sisters, I remember laughing so hard that milk came out my nose. This would, of course, produce even bigger laughs around the table. And more milk. Sometimes I literally could *not* stop laughing, until the sobering words of my mother—"You're *still* going to finish your dinner!"—got to me. When I got older and developed an interest in performing, my folks allowed me to be the after-dinner entertainment. Sometimes we had to tie my little sister to a chair so she wouldn't walk out during my show.

Eating and laughing go well together: Restaurants can be ridiculous; fast food is funny. If you want to perplex a fast-food worker, respond to the big question "Will this be for here or to go?" by answering, "To go here."

Read this chapter and then, over dinner, share some of the humorous cooking tips, eating-out ideas, or a verse or two of poetic nonsense with a friend or family member. Offer them a glass of milk. Then be sure to back away from the table.

• • •

Appetite Suppressants

The lady at Burger King told me I could have it my way.
So I left and went to Wendy's.
—*Scott Wood*

I can't cook. I use a smoke alarm as a timer.
—*Carol Siskind*

The coffee business is getting so ridiculous. There's a
new coffee company that delivers overnight. It's called
Federal Espresso.

—*Bill Jones*

Never eat in a restaurant where you see a cockroach
bench-pressing a burrito.
—*Pat McCormick*

Q: What's a dude's favorite candy?
A: Milk Dudes.
—*Nick Arnette*

He dreamed he was eating Shredded Wheat and woke
up to find the mattress half gone.
—*Fred Allen*

I guess the Big Gulp at 7-Eleven wasn't big enough. Now they have the "Super Double" Gulp. Seventy-two ounces of soda. It comes with its own lifeguard. I looked inside the cup; they were filming an episode of *Baywatch* in there.

—Scott Wood

Hunger Pains

Shake and shake the catsup bottle:
None will come, and then a lot'll.
—Richard Armour

There used to be a popular restaurant in Pittsburg called Captain Cook's. The owner, Barney Cook, was a real clown and cutup. He was always playing practical jokes and cheering everybody up. Barney had a loudspeaker and would announce every customer's name as they came in.

One day, one of Barney's friends, Joe the mailman, came by, and while he was eating dinner, he suddenly slumped over on the floor. Joe's face turned blue, and he was gasping for breath, like he was having a heart attack.

Everybody panicked. People were running around calling for a doctor, a nurse, an ambulance. Barney calmly told everyone to move aside. He got down on his hands and knees, and whispered in the man's ear: "Joe, can you hear me?"

"Yeah, I can hear you," Joe replied weakly.

"Have you paid your check?" Barney asked.

Joe started laughing—and laughing and laughing. A healthy color returned to his face, and by the time the ambulance arrived, Joe was up and assured everyone he was feeling fine.

—*The Joyful Noiseletter*

Q. What did the yogi say to the hot-dog vendor?

A. Make me one with everything.

—*Vogue magazine*

Why is it that lemon pie filling and lemonade are made with "artificial lemon flavoring," but dish soap and furniture polish are made with real lemon juice?

—*Bruce Johnson*

I think humans complain too much. People who don't like seafood complain that it tastes too fishy. Only a human would be so arrogant as to eat something and then complain it tastes like *itself*!!

—*Brad Stine*

I think the people who work at McDonald's know that the food is bad. I bought my nephew a Happy Meal. The prize inside was a roll of Tums.

—*Scott Wood*

A hamburger by any other name costs twice as much.
—*The Humor Gazette*

We have a new recipe for an exotic gourmet dinner:
"First take two credit cards . . ."
—*Bessie and Beulah*

Cured ham? No, thanks, pal. Cured of what? What if it
has a relapse on my plate?
—*Tommy Sledge*

I'm really upset with the restaurant parking
attendants. . . . They won't validate my feelings.
—*Scott Wood*

Corn flakes facedown on the kitchen floor
Raisin Bran blood in the cellar
And a note near the Grape Nuts
Smashed on the door
This was the work of the Cereal Killer.
—*Adam Christing*

Holy Bible Humor

The One whose throne is in heaven sits laughing. . . .
—Psalm 2:4

A grumpy philosopher was reading the Scriptures to his six-year-old grandson. He got to the verse that says, "Why do you stare at the speck of dust in your friend's eye and pay no attention to the log sticking out of your own eye?" His little grandson starting chuckling, and the man's first thought was How dare you laugh at the Bible?

Then he realized that Jesus was employing an amusing exaggeration. He went on to find about thirty other examples of Christ's use of humor. Outlandish sarcasm is sprinkled throughout the Bible: In the Old Testament, when Gideon was hiding from his enemies in a wine press, the Angel of the Lord appeared to him saying, "Oh, Valiant Warrior."

The Bible condones a good laugh. Proverbs says, "A merry heart doeth good like medicine." So go back to the beginning and have a laugh with Adam and Eve, Moses, and Pharaoh.

• • •

I feel sorry for Moses. He spent forty years wandering the desert, eating nothing but bread off the ground and the occasional bird, and every day a million people would come up to him and ask, "Are we there yet?!"
—*Robert G. Lee*

It seems such a pity that Noah and his party did not miss the boat.
—*Mark Twain*

I think Adam had the most pressure. He had to name all the animals . . . by himself. Most people have nine months to come up with one baby name they both like; he had one day to come up with *nine million* animal names!
—*Brad Stine*

Until Eve arrived, this was a man's world.
—*Richard Armour*

The Song of Solomon is the one book of the Bible dedicated solely to romantic love. Isn't it ironic that its initials are SOS?
—*Paul McGinty*

Peter remained on friendly terms with Christ notwithstanding Christ's having healed his mother-in-law.
—*Nicholas Murray Butler*

BIBLE = Basic Instructions Before Leaving Earth.
—*Sunday school teacher*

The Bible tells us to love our neighbors, and also to love our enemies; probably because they are generally the same people.
—*Gilbert Keith Chesterton*

As for evolution, I have a hard time believing that billions of years ago two protozoan bumped into each other under a volcanic cesspool and evolved into Cindy Crawford.
—*Robert G. Lee*

MINISTER: Do you know what's in the Bible?
LITTLE GIRL: Yes. I think I know everything that's in it.
MINISTER: You do? Tell me.
LITTLE GIRL: OK. There's a picture of my brother's girlfriend, a ticket from the dry cleaners, one of my curls, and a Pizza Hut coupon.
—*Mark Brown*

The shortest poem ever written is about fleas in the Garden of Eden:
Adam
Had 'em.
—*H. Alan Dunn*

They have the Bible on compact disc now. It's sixty-eight discs made by a company in Redondo Beach, California. It's the King Dude's translation. You put it on and hear:

"In the beginning, there was, like, nada. And God separated the land and the water and made surf. And on the seventh day, there were some gnarly waves, dude!"

Moses runs into Pharaoh: "This captivity's bogus! Let us go, Sand-man!"

Mary comes in: "He is risen, I am, like, so sure!"

It's, like, a great Bible. But sixty-eight discs? This is just a little overkill, don't you think? Are you going to listen to it? I don't think so. You're going to put it on in the background of a party and people are going to mill around and then say, "Is that Sermon on the Mount? I haven't heard that one in ages!"

But if you really want to freak them out, put it on random play. "Wow. Did you know Mary gave birth to Elijah, who was swallowed by a whale, then killed by the jawbone of a donkey? I'd better brush up on my Bible."

—Robert G. Lee

The first pair ate the first apple.
—Anonymous

What a good thing Adam had: When he said a good thing, he knew nobody had said it before.
—Mark Twain

Some people have a hard time believing that all of those animals could fit inside Noah's ark. But what amazes me is that Noah built the ark without a single power tool.

—Bill Jones

In biblical days it was considered a miracle for a donkey to speak; now it would be a miracle if one kept quiet.

—H. Alan Dunn

It's hard being human. Look at the prototypes, Adam and Eve. That's a lot of pressure, being the first people. You make one mistake, *everybody* hears about it. You're constantly answering embarrassing questions about how you messed up: "Okay, for the five millionth time, I was sitting around, minding my own business, and she goes . . . 'Want a bite?'"

—Brad Stine

Authorship

King David and King Solomon
Led merry, merry lives,
With many, many lady friends
And many, many wives;
But when old age crept over them,
With many, many qualms,
King Solomon wrote the Proverbs
And King David wrote the Psalms.

—James Naylor

Kiddin' Around

*Any kid will run an errand for you,
if you ask him at bedtime.*
—Red Skelton

Kids say the darndest things. Ask Art Linkletter. And some of their favorite jokes are pretty good, too. Like world clown Bruce "Charlie" Johnson's popular "Why did the turtle cross the road?" Answer: "To get to the Shell station."

Brilliantly funny statements are kids' stock in trade: When you ask a little kid what he wants to be when he grows up, you may hear something like "A fire truck."

In this chapter, you'll find wonderfully funny statements from and about children. Out of the mouths of babes often comes—oatmeal.

• • •

During summer vacation, our children were looking forward to visiting the Grand Canyon. Once there, our ten-year-old son marveled at the vastness of the canyon. But our four-year-old daughter kept looking around, and after fifteen minutes she said, "Daddy, I see a big hole in the ground, now show me the *Grand Crayon*."
—John Hakel

78

Last spring my son and I planted tomatoes in our backyard. A few months later he was so amazed they actually grew, he said we must have a "Gardening Angel."

—*Robert G. Lee*

Adults are always asking little kids what they want to be when they grow up—'cause they're looking for ideas.

—*Paula Poundstone*

I stopped believing in Santa Claus when I was six. Mother took me to see him in a department store and he asked for my autograph.

—*Shirley Temple*

Indifference

When Grandmamma fell off the boat,
And couldn't swim (and wouldn't float),
Matilda just stood by and smiled.
I almost could have slapped the child.

—*Harry Graham*

During this past Christmas while I was on a shopping spree in a department store I heard a little five-year-old talking to his mother on the down escalator. He said, "Mommy, what do they do when the basement gets full of steps?"

—*Hal Linden*

Children make the most desirable opponents in Scrabble as they are both easy to beat and fun to cheat.
—*Fran Lebowitz*

Our three-year-old daughter looked at a calendar and asked, "How many *be good* days until Christmas?"
—*John Hakel*

We should not tell our kids they can be whatever they want to be. We should ask them, "What will you settle for?" You want to be a fireman? How about working as a short order cook at Sizzler? There *are* flames involved.
—*Robert G. Lee*

Q. What kind of shampoo do Siamese twins use?
A. Extra body!
—*Shiloh Ahlstrand*

Our four-year-old Candice inquired, "When our goldfish die could we take them out and eat them?"
—*Bobbi Bourbonnais*

What's the first thing a little girl wants when she gets a new bike? *A basket*—she's prepared to shop. What's the first thing a boy wants on his bike? *A bell or horn*—he's prepared for traffic. What's the first toy a little girl wants? *A doll*—she's prepared to shop with friends. What's

the first toy a little boy wants? *A gun*—he's prepared for traffic.
—*Jason Chase*

Batman got his name because he fell into a bat cave as a young boy. Good thing he didn't fall into an elephant cave.
—*Paul McGinty*

When Maria, the daughter of William Howard Taft III, was a shy schoolgirl, she was asked by her teacher for a brief family history. This is what Maria wrote:

```
My great-grandfather was President of the
United States.

My grandfather was Senator from Ohio. My fa-
ther is Ambassador to Ireland. I am a Brownie.

                                       Maria
```

—*Dear Wit*

With our first child, I must admit I wasn't prepared for the hospital sticker shock. My wife did all the work, but the hospital still charged us over $5,000. I couldn't afford that, so we had to put our daughter on layaway.
—*Robert G. Lee*

I'll never forget the excitement when Grandpa shaved off his beard . . . and we found out it was Grandma.
—*Gerald F. Lieberman*

Laugh After Death

If you're not allowed to laugh in heaven,
I don't want to go there.
—Martin Luther

Comedy and tragedy are kissin' cousins. It really depends on your perspective: Some people's philosophy is "Life is hard. Then you die." But you can also believe that life is filled with joy and then you go to heaven (unless you're attending an atheist's funeral, looking at somebody who's all dressed up with no place to go).

I once performed for an association of morticians. I thought it would be a tough gig. But they understood that life is too short not to have a few laughs.

So live it up. Share this stuff with friends. They'll *die.* You will enjoy the outrageous things celebrities, politicians, ministers, humorists, and even tombstones have had to say about the grin reaper. Sorry about the puns. I know, I know. This is a grave matter.

• • •

For three days after death, hair and fingernails
continue to grow but phone calls taper off.
—Johnny Carson

My uncle's funeral cost $5,000 so far. We buried him
in a rented tuxedo.
—*Dave Madden*

How come every time you go to the emergency room of
a hospital they got foreign doctors from India there?
I don't want to put my life in the hands of any doctor
who believes in reincarnation. Give me a good old-
fashioned American doc who'll make sure you live to
pay that bill!
—*Glen Super*

"God is dead."
—Nietzsche, 1886
"Nietzsche is dead."
—God, 1900
—*Bumper sticker*

I do benefits for all religions—I'd hate to blow the
hereafter on a technicality.
—*Bob Hope*

Heaven goes by favor; if it went by merit, you would
stay out and your dog would go in.
—*Mark Twain*

If you don't go to people's funerals,
they won't come to yours.
—*Anonymous*

I don't want to tell you how much insurance I carry with the Prudential, but all I can say is: When I go, *they* go.

—*Jack Benny*

I am ready to meet my Maker. Whether my Maker is prepared for the ordeal of meeting me is another matter.

—*Winston Churchill (on his eightieth birthday)*

Death: to stop sinning suddenly.

—*Elbert Hubbard*

Where there's a will, there's a lawsuit.

—*Addison Mizner*

When I die, I'm going to leave my body to science fiction.

—*Steven Wright*

As for reincarnation, I have a hard time believing in any religion that says you have to go through puberty again.

—*Robert G. Lee*

Mark Twain once went to a dinner party where the chief subject of conversation was talk about eternal life and future punishment. Twain sat in silence through-out the conversation. Finally a woman asked, "Why do you not say anything? I would like to hear your opinion."

"Madam, you must excuse me," Twain replied. "I am silent of necessity—I have friends in both places."
—*The Joyful Noiseletter*

If I am ever stuck out on a respirator or a life-support system, I definitely want to be unplugged—but not till I get down to a size 8.
—*Henriette Mantel*

My cousin's into reincarnation. She claims that she was there at the birth of Christ. It seems that anybody who's into this stuff claims to have seen Christ. Bethlehem must've been packed! That's why there was no room at the inn; my cousin had advance reservations.
—*Robert G. Lee*

I believe in reincarnation. I've had other lives. I know.
I have clues. First of all, I'm exhausted.
—*Carol Siskind*

They say such nice things about people at their funerals that it makes me sad to realize that I'm going to miss mine by just a few days.
—*Garrison Keillor*

If you can read this, you're too close; get off my grave, idiot!
—*Glen Super*

I Would Rather Be Living in Philadelphia.
—*W. C. Fields*

I told you I was ill.
—*Spike Mulligan*

Keep the line moving.
—*Jack Paar*

Looked up the elevator shaft to see if the car was coming down. It was.
—*Harry Edsel Smith's gravestone*

The tombstone is about the only thing that can stand upright and lie on its face at the same time.

—*Mary Wilson Little*

Epitaph: a belated advertisement for a line of goods that has been permanently discontinued.

—*Irvin Shrewsbury Cobb*

My mother always said that every time you do a good deed here on earth, you're storing up a treasure in heaven. Which means Mother Teresa's probably got some beachfront property up there and I'm up to a box of Milk Duds and a Pez dispenser.

—*Robert G. Lee*

A woman died and went to heaven. At the pearly gates, St. Peter was quizzing the new arrivals. "Before you may enter, can you tell me God's first name?" he asked.

After thinking a moment, the woman smiled and said, "Andy!"

"Andy?" St. Peter replied. "Where'd you get Andy?"

"We sang it in church all the time: 'Andy walks with me, Andy talks with me, Andy tells me I am His own. . . .'"

—*The Joyful Noiseletter*

I'm not afraid of dying. I just don't want to be there when it happens.

—*Woody Allen*

Momusements

Having a baby is like taking your lower lip and forcing it over your head.
—Carol Burnett

My mom used to say, "I don't know what I'd do without you kids. But I'd sure like to know." She was just teasing us. I think. I remember hiding vegetables in my socks so I wouldn't have to eat them. My mom would catch me and make me eat the veggies and the socks. Mom was the first one to make you smile. And she probably laughed the very moment you were born (so did the doctor). In these great one- and two-liners about mothers, I was careful to select material only from funny folks who are or who have had mothers.

Hopefully your mom, or your mom-in-law, won't mind a bit of ribbing. If she does, don't worry about it. Just give her the greatest gift a mother can receive from her child: guilt.

• • •

I haven't spoken to my mother-in-law for eighteen months—I don't like to interrupt her.
—Ken Dodd

MOTHER: Do you love me, Albert?

ALBERT: Yes.

MOTHER: Yes—what?

ALBERT: Yes, please.

—Tom Stoppard

My mom's using a new face cream for Jewish women.
It's called Oil of Oy Vay.

—Scott Wood

The Rose Bowl is the only bowl I've ever seen that I
didn't have to clean.

—Erma Bombeck

We just had a surprise party for my mom's sixty-fifth
birthday. She was completely surprised . . . because
she's fifty!

—Brad Stine

My mother said, "You won't amount to anything
because you procrastinate." I said, "Just wait."

—Judy Tenuta

Q. What do you have when your mother-in-law drives
off a cliff in your brand new BMW?
A. Mixed emotions.

—Curtis Mitchell

I idolized my mother. I didn't realize she was a lousy cook until I went into the Army.
—Jackie Gayle

Never lend your car to anyone to whom you have given birth.
—Erma Bombeck

I have found that no kisses can ever compare to "mom" kisses, because mom kisses can heal anything. You can have a hangnail, a broken heart, or catatonic schizophrenia; with moms, one kiss and you're fine.
—Robert G. Lee

My mother loved children—she would have given anything if I had been one.
—Groucho Marx

I was always getting punished as a kid. Even at birth my mom put me on restriction . . . She blamed me for breaking her water!
—Scott Wood

A woman came to ask the doctor if a woman should have children after thirty-five. I said thirty-five children is enough for any woman!
—Gracie Allen

My mom used to tell me not to eat so fast because it wasn't good for me. So I put a strobe light over the table.
—*Nick Arnette*

Few mistakes can be made by a mother-in-law who is willing to baby-sit.
—*The Humor Gazette*

Mother Doesn't Want a Dog

Mother doesn't want a dog.
Mother says they smell,
And never sit when you say sit,
Or even when you yell.
And when you come home late at night
And there is ice and snow,
You have to go back out because
The dumb dog has to go.

Mother doesn't want a dog.
Mother says they shed,
And always let the strangers in
And bark at friends instead,
And do disgraceful things on rugs,
And track mud on the floor,
And flop upon your bed at night
And snore their doggy snore.

Mother doesn't want a dog.
She's making a mistake.
Because, more than a dog, I think
She will not want this snake.
—*Judith Viorst*

Daditudes

Dads are born without the sympathy gene. You can break your leg, hobble into your house, and all your dad will do is look over the paper and grumble, "Shake it off!"
—Robert G. Lee

One Christmas, when I was five years old, I noticed that my new bicycle wasn't put together right. I asked my dad about it. "Don't Santa's helpers know how to fix everything?" My dad answered, "There is no Santa." Dads aren't always known for their sensitivity. Sometimes they can be so blunt, their words cut to the funny bone. Like when funny guy Steve Pearl phoned his dad to tell him he stopped smoking. His dad called him a quitter.

Fortunately, fathers can usually handle being made fun of—when they catch the joke, that is. This chapter consists of uproarious stories, jokes, and remarks about dear old dad.

• • •

My son has taken up meditation—at least it's better than sitting doing nothing.
—*Max Kauffmann*

When you're a parent you become an idiot. It's not our fault. It's the television shows we watch. I used to watch the news. Now I watch *Sesame Street* and *Mr. Rogers.*

I wanted to buy a car, determined to give the salesman a run for his money. I had forgotten: I'm an idiot. I walked up to him and said,

"The car is nice. The look is handsome. But the price you ask: a king's ransom. There is no need for me to stay. I will not buy this car today."

Wait a minute, I thought, I just became Dr. Seuss there for a second! The salesman was obviously a parent because he said,

"Would you? Could you? On a dare, buy this car with factory air? If I throw in a music box, would you buy this Audi Fox?"

I said, "I would not, could not on a dare, I do not want your factory air. I would not buy it in the rain. I would not buy it on a train. Not in a house. Not in a mouse. Not in a goat. Not in a moat. I don't care if it runs on Green Eggs and Ham, I will not buy it Sam I Am!"
—*Robert G. Lee*

My dad was the town drunk. A lot of times that's not so bad—but New York City?
—*Henny Youngman*

A tornado touched down, uprooting a large tree in the front yard and demolishing the house across the street. Dad went to the door, opened it, surveyed the damage, muttered "Darn kids!" and closed the door.
—*Tim Conway*

He read in the paper that it takes ten dollars a year to support a kid in India. So he sent his kids there.

—*Red Buttons*

When I was a kid I said to my father one afternoon, "Daddy, will you take me to the zoo?" He answered, "If the zoo wants you, let them come and get you."

—*Jerry Lewis*

I have found the best way to give advice to your children is to find out what they want and then advise them to do it.

—*Harry S. Truman*

My father used tell me, "When Abraham Lincoln was your age, Abraham Lincoln had a job. When Abraham Lincoln was your age, he walked twelve miles to get to school." I said, "Dad, when Lincoln was your age, he was President, okay?"

—*Andy Andrews*

My dad used to play fun games with me as a child. "Guess who's adopted." "Pet the pit bull." "Dodge bomb."

—*Scott Wood*

A girl of about sixteen won as a prize a trip to Washington. She was introduced to Mr. Coolidge; as she shook hands with him, she said, "Mr. President, my father bet me ten dollars I wouldn't get three words out of you." Mr.

Coolidge looked at her without batting an eye, and said, "Dad wins."
—*Rev. James Whitcomb Brougher, Sr.*

When you have a baby, people around you get very stupid. I was walking my daughter in a stroller in the park when this woman came up and started gushing all over her, "Oh, look at the cute little baby! Such a cute little baby! Where did you ever get such a cute little baby?" I told her, "At the corner gas station, they're giving them away with every fill-up."
—*Robert G. Lee*

As a kid, I thought my dad was blind and deaf. He would sit for hours in his recliner moaning, "I can't see! I wish I could hear what's going on!" Finally my mom told me to quiet down and to stop playing in front of the TV.
—*Adam Christing*

My dad's a writer. His favorite expression is "The pen is mightier than the sword," which I believed for a long time. Until I moved into the city. And I got into a fight with this guy. He cut me up real bad, and I drew a mustache on his face. And then I wrote him a nasty letter.
—*Kevin Brennan*

I am your father. I brought you into this world, and I can take you out.
—*Cliff Huxtable,* The Cosby Show

When it came to spankings, my dad never used a belt. One time he grabbed a piece of my Hot Wheels race car track. In my mind I'm thinking, Great, now I'm being beat with my own toys. . . .

Thank God I didn't get that wood burning set I wanted.

—*Scott Wood*

Sporting a Grin

*Iraq attacks Kuwait; there's an upheaval in Liberia;
there's an attempted coup in the Philippines.
You get the feeling that the Goodwill Games just
didn't work out last year.*
—Jay Leno

There's an awful lot of humor in sports: making fun of
the rival team, watching sports bloopers, examining
special quirks of our favorite game. Golf, for example, is
self-defeating and may be the most frustrating sport of
all (which is why there are so many golf jokes). Bill
Cosby said, "You got the ball. You had it right there. Then
you hit it away! And then you go and walk after it again!
It's a dumb game." If you are a golfer, here are several
vintage golf jokes that will get some big laughs in the
clubhouse.

But no matter what your game—bowling, football,
boxing, even bungee jumping—you'll find something
here to laugh at.

• • •

Professional sports are getting so violent. Next season
they're having Monday Night Drive-By Football.
—*Bill Jones*

Harry and his wife had been playing golf for many years at a rustic, rural course which lay beside a beautiful stretch of farmland. One day on the difficult par four 16th hole, Harry hooked his drive so far to the left of the fairway that he was faced with an extraordinarily difficult second shot. A huge red barn lay between his ball and the green. However, Harry's wife noticed that the barn doors were open, and she said, "Harry, if you'll punch a two iron real low I think you can hit it right through the open barn doors and reach the green in two."

Harry sized up the shot and agreed with his wife. He took a two iron from his bag and hit the shot low. But the ball slammed against the side of the barn and ricocheted directly backward, striking his wife in the forehead and killing her instantly. He was so distraught he quit playing golf for years.

Finally, at the urging of friends, Harry returned to the game. One day he was playing the same treacherous 16th hole with a friend. Once again his tee shot went astray, far left of the fairway.

Harry's friend helped him line up the shot and suggested, "Harry, if you'll punch a two iron real low I think you can hit it through the open barn doors and reach the green in two."

This advice moved Harry to tears. "Are you kidding?" he said in disgust. "The last time I tried that shot here I took a double-bogey."

—*Paul D. Brown*

Golf is a good walk spoiled.
—*Mark Twain*

Cheerleaders at football games have jackets that say "Cheerleader" on the back of them. I guess that's so you can tell them apart from the sixty-year-old man selling peanuts.

—Nick Arnette

I fish, therefore I lie.

—T-shirt

My mom is eighty years old and still bowling. Yesterday she got three strikes. One was even in her lane.

—Scott Wood

Athlete: a dignified bunch of muscles, unable to do dishes or mow the lawn.

—H. Alan Dunn

A guy is standing in front of his locker at the country club admiring a golf ball he has in his hand. One of his golfing buddies says to him, "What'd you do, get some new golf balls?" And the guy says, "Would you believe that this is the greatest golf ball ever made. You can't lose it. You hit it into the rough and it whistles. You hit it into the woods and a bell inside goes off. If you drive it into a lake, a big burst of steam shoots up six feet in the air for two minutes." And his friend says, "That's great. Where did you get it?" And the guy says, "I found it."

—Soupy Sales

I left because of illness and fatigue—
the fans were sick and tired of me.
—*John Ralston, former coach of the Denver Broncos*

Whoever invented bungee jumping must have watched
a lot of *Road Runner* cartoons.
—*Nick Arnette*

Every decade or so, I attempted to play tennis, and it always consists of thirty-seven seconds of actually hitting the ball and two hours of yelling, "Where did the ball go?" "Over that condominium!" With bowling, once you let go of the ball, it's no longer your legal responsibility. They have these wonderful machines that find it for you and send it right back.
—*Dave Barry*

I put Sugar Ray Robinson on the canvas—when he
tripped over my body.
—*Rocky Graziano*

A: Why aren't you playing golf with the colonel any more?
B: What! Would *you* play with a man who swears and curses with every shot, who cheats in the bunkers, and who enters false scores on his cards?
A: Certainly not!
B: Well, neither will the colonel.
—*Freddie Oliver*

Jim was just beginning to make a putt when a funeral procession drove by the golf course. He bowed his head, holding his hat over his heart until the procession had passed, then he began putting again. His golf buddies said, "Wow, Jim, we had no idea you were a religious person. . . . That was very sensitive!" He replied, "Well, after all, I *was* married to her for twenty-eight years!"

—Pete McLeod

Age Rage

You know you're getting older when you like
to see the cops go by.
—Jason Chase

When an old man told his friend he had purchased a new hearing aid, his friend asked, "What kind is it?" The old man answered, "About four-thirty."

We're not getting any younger, but that's okay. Take a walk on the lighter side. Laughter does wonders for your sense of well-being. Try this experiment without chuckling if you can: Stand up, put a big smile on your face—even if it's a fake, plastic one—and look straight up. Now, *feel bad.* It's hard, isn't it? It's not easy to feel bad when you're looking up. So take a break and enjoy the wholesome, timeless comedy of Ed Wynn, Red Skelton, and Lucille Ball.

• • •

The secret to staying young is to live honestly, eat
slowly, and lie about your age.
—*Lucille Ball*

Middle age occurs when you are too young to take up
golf and too old to rush up to the net.
—*Franklin Pierce Adams*

There are three ages of man: youth, middle age, and "gee, you look good." But I don't let old age bother me. There are three signs of old age. Loss of memory . . . I forget the other two.

—*Red Skelton*

PATIENT: Doctor, I think I'm suffering from lack of memory.
DOCTOR: How long have you had this problem?
PATIENT: What problem is that?

—*Mark Brown*

He's so old he gets winded playing checkers.
—*Ed Wynn*

I'm older than most comedians. I take audiences back. Way back. Back to the fifties. Back when women wore their underwear beneath their clothes. Back when girls wore earrings and guys wore jockey shorts. So far back, sushi was called bait.

—*Jason Chase*

Quit worrying about your health. . . .
It will go away.
—*Harry Allen*

There's one thing about children—they never go around showing snapshots of their grandparents.
—*Bessie and Beulah*

My doctor said I look like a million dollars—
green and wrinkled.
—*Red Skelton*

Middle age is when your age starts to show
around your middle.
—*Bob Hope*

To me, old age is always fifteen years older than I am.
—*Bernard Baruch*

An archaeologist is the best husband a woman can have; the older she gets, the more interested he is in her.

—*Agatha Christie (she was married to one)*

You know you're getting old, there are certain signs. I walked past a cemetery and two guys ran after me with shovels.

—*Rodney Dangerfield*

PATIENT: I just turned forty and I've been having strange dreams.

PSYCHOLOGIST: What have you been dreaming?

PATIENT: I keep dreaming that I'm living in a tepee or stuck inside a wigwam. What do you make of it?

PSYCHOLOGIST: I think you are two tents.
—*Anonymous*

Learning thru Laughter

Old principals never die; they just lose their faculties.
—Harry Allen

For a lot of us, it was the fun times that got us through the hard knocks of growing up and going to school. In junior high, I ran for student body president. My campaign speech was a monologue full of jokes and one-liners. My very serious opponent then asked the students, "Do you want to elect a *clown* for president?" Of course, I won.

These days, students have a very short attention span, but they are still posing deep, relevant questions, like What do you call a dog with no front legs? (Answer: Scooter.)

Laughter is conducive to learning. Your assignment: Read these clever quips, questions, and quotations from the wisest of men, like Winston Churchill, and the deepest of dudes, like Nick Arnette.

• • •

Class Clowns . . .

TEACHER: Which is a bigger problem for young people today, lack of knowledge or apathy?

STUDENT: I don't know and I don't care.

—*Anonymous*

Nietzsche's peachy
but Sartre's smarter
—*Ogden Nash*

Q: What do you call a dude you think you've seen before?
A: A Déjà Dude.
—*Nick Arnette*

I just got out of the hospital. I was in a speed-reading accident. I hit a bookmark.
—*Steven Wright*

What's on your mind—if you'll forgive the overstatement?
—*Fred Allen*

Q: Why do Jews answer a question with a question?
A: Why shouldn't Jews answer a question with a question?
—*Anonymous*

There are 70 million books in American libraries, but
the one you want to read is always out.
—*Tom Masson*

Higher Intelligence

A fellow told me he was going to hang-glider school. He
said, "I've been going for three months." I said, "How
many successful jumps do you need to make before
you graduate?" He said, "All of them."
—*Red Skelton*

"Whom are you?" said he, for he had been
to night school.
—*George Ade*

Q: What do you call a dyslexic dude?
A: Edud.
—*Nick Arnette*

Don't be so open-minded that your brains fall out.
—*Josh McDowell*

History will be kind to me, for I intend to write it.
—*Winston Churchill*

Bad Spellers of the world UNTIE!
—*Button*

The covers of this book are too far apart.
—*Ambrose Bierce*

How do seedless grapes reproduce?
—*Mark Matlock*

Student excuses of the future:
A.) Please excuse Johnny from school today; we're trading him in for a more lifelike droid.
B.) Teacher: "Billy, where's your book?"
Billy: "What's a book?"
C.) My dog reprogrammed my homework.
—*Nick Arnette*

Illiterate? Write for help.
—*Bumper sticker*

Musical Comedy

The Beatles said, "All you need is love."
And then they broke up.
—Larry Norman

In 1962 a Decca Records executive refused to offer the Beatles a recording contract. He said, "We don't like their sound. Groups of guitars are on the way out." With that kind of discernment, he probably went on to become a music critic.

Music can have a soothing effect on the soul (unless you play it backwards). But sometimes it sounds absurd. Like when you're attending a musical at the theater and suddenly, for no apparent reason, a character in the play bursts out in song. I don't get it.

Here are a few nutty lines of musical mirth, roasting the Rolling Stones, opera, accordion players, school band leaders, and more.

• • •

I don't know anything about music.
In my line you don't have to.
—Elvis Presley

In the seventies, Satan's big trick was backward-masking. He hid secret messages on record albums. I figure, if you listen to records backwards, you *deserve* to hear a message from Satan.
—Brad Stine

Comedy premise one hundred years in the future: "So, I was at the Rolling Stones farewell tour. . . ."
—Nick Arnette

Sleep is an excellent way of listening to an opera.
—James Stephens

A good musical comedy consists largely of disorderly conduct occasionally interrupted by talk.
—George Ade

Opera is when a guy gets stabbed in the back and instead of bleeding he sings.
—Ed Gardner

Use an accordion, go to jail! That's the law!
—Bumper sticker

I've never heard such corny lyrics, such simpering sentimentality, such repetitious, uninspired melody. Man, we've got a hit on our hands!
—Brad Anderson

Perhaps it was because Nero played the fiddle,
they burned Rome.
—*Oliver Herford*

I played in the school band in junior high. I was always
a beat behind because of following the conductor's
wand. I was following the flab underneath his arms.
—*Nick Arnette*

I hate music, especially when it's played.
—*Jimmy Durante*

I used to be a dancer, but the music
would throw me off.
—*Anonymous*

Once in every lifetime a really beautiful song comes
along . . . Until it does, I'd like to do this one.
—*Cliff Richard (pop singer)*

Smoke Signals

I don't smoke, I never have, I don't even understand what the point of it is. All I can tell is that these people are addicted to blowing smoke out of their faces. It's not even a good *trick. Now, if you could blow smoke out of your face without everyone knowing where it came from, that* would be impressive.
—Brad Stine

I remember the first time I smoked a cigarette. I was about ten years old. My friend and I hid in a bush in my front yard. We didn't quite know how to light up, so we lit some leaves on fire to ignite our smokes. The resulting burning bush experience nearly burned down the whole neighborhood.

These days, smokers are beginning to feel like an endangered species. So here are some pro-smoking remarks, along with the thoughts of a few soft-spoken nonsmokers, like Brad Stine. I'm trying to be neutral here. Just like the tobacco companies.

• • •

Puffed Up

Smoking is, as far as I'm concerned, the entire point of being an adult.
—*Fran Lebowitz*

I have made it a rule never to smoke more than one cigar at a time.
—*Mark Twain*

Many smokers die of lung cancer. Anti-smoking activists die of stress-related heart attacks.
—*Bill Jones*

I never smoked a cigarette until I was nine.
—*W.C. Fields*

Most people who smoke will eventually contract a fatal disease and die. But they don't brag about it, do they? Most people who ski, play professional football, or drive race cars, will not die—at least not in the act—and yet they are the ones with the glamorous images, the expensive equipment, and the mythic proportions. Why this should be I cannot say, unless it is simply that the average American does not know a daredevil when he sees one.
—*Fran Lebowitz*

Tobacco is a dirty weed. I like it,
It satisfies no normal need. I like it,
It makes you thin, it makes you lean,
It takes the hair right off your bean
It's the worst darn stuff I've ever seen.
I like it.
——*Graham Lee Hemminger*

What a Drag

Cigarette packaging amazes me. How would anyone fall for some of the rhetoric? "Light" cigarettes. What does this mean? You get "light" cancer? Are surgeons relieved? "We found a tumor . . . but, it's as light as a Wiffle ball!"
——*Brad Stine*

Smokers should have a place where only they can shop. We could call it "The Pall Mall." There would be lovely stores: The GAsP, SOOT Locker, HACKery Farms.
——*Nick Arnette*

I started smoking to lose weight. After I dropped that lung I felt pretty good.
——*Michael Meehan*

I've taken up smoking. My doctor says I'm not getting enough tar in my diet.
—*Steve Martin*

It seems to me the uses of tobacco aren't obvious right off the bat. You can shred it up and put it on a piece of paper and roll it up and stick it between your lips . . . and then you set fire to it! Then what do you do? You inhale the smoke. It seems offhand you could stand in front of your fireplace and have the same thing going.
—*Bob Newhart*

As ye smoke, so shall ye reek.
—*Anonymous*

What bothers me is smokers who don't take responsibility for their own actions. Claiming ignorance: "I started smoking when I was a kid and now I can't stop!" Yeah, I used to wet my pants when I was younger. . . . I got over it.
—*Brad Stine*

The only way to stop smoking is to just stop—no ifs, ands, or butts.
—*Edith Zittler*

Belly Laughs

The second day of a diet is always easier than the first.
By the second day you're off it.
—Jackie Gleason

What are you supposed to do? Commercials send you mixed messages. "Lose weight now!" "You'll feel like eating the whole bag of our tasty chips!" If you took commercials seriously, you'd expect yourself to eat like a pig and look like a model.

One day I came to the realization that I love food more than fitness. I think it was when my daughter asked me, "Daddy, are you pregnant?" At the time of this writing, I'm on a new diet. I'm taking Miss Piggy's advice to "Never eat more than you can lift."

If you have ever wanted to shape up, this chapter is for you. It will help you feel full. Okay, maybe not. But these exercise, health, and diet jokes will make you roll with laughter—which probably burns some calories. Still feeling fat? Laugh it off.

• • •

The two biggest sellers in any bookstore are the cookbooks and the diet books. The cookbooks tell you how to prepare the food and the diet books tell you how not to eat any of it.

—Andy Rooney

I got hit by a Volkswagen—and had to go to the hospital to have it removed.

—*Pat McCormick*

Richard Simmons has a new workout video for senior citizens. It's called "Collapsing to the Oldies."

—*Scott Wood*

Begged an irritable lady at a tea party:

Please diet
In quiet.

—*Bennett Cerf*

You can't lose weight without exercise. But I've got a philosophy about exercise. I don't think you should punish your legs for something your mouth did. Drag your lips around the block once or twice.

—*Guy Owen*

My wife and I burned out four refrigerator lights since Christmas. We have a sign on the fridge which says "We Never Close."

—*Jason Chase*

Did you ever see the customers in health-food stores? They are pale, skinny people who look half-dead. In a steak house, you see robust, ruddy people. They're dying, of course, but they look terrific.

—*Bill Cosby*

I joined a health spa recently. They had a sign for "Free Weights." So I took a couple.
—*Scott Wood*

Whenever I feel like exercise, I lie down until the feeling passes.
—*Robert Hutchins*

She had a lot of fat that did not fit.
—*Herbert George Wells*

I've been on every diet in the world. The best one is the BBC diet: Buy Bigger Clothes!
—*Guy Owen*

Chubby girls are more fun than skinny girls. You go to a skinny girl's house, you're lucky to get mineral water and sprouts. You go to a chubby girl's house, *you know there's food there.*

And chubby girls give the best directions. If you want to know how to get somewhere, ask a chubby girl. "Okay. You go up the street till you see the big Wendy's. Turn right and go past the McDonald's. There's a Colonel Sanders. Make a left . . ."
—*Jason Chase*

I'm not working out. My philosophy: No pain, no pain.
—*Carol Leifer*

The only way to keep your health is to eat what you don't want, drink what you don't like, and do what you'd rather not.

—*Mark Twain*

I tried Flintstones vitamins. I didn't feel any better but I could stop the car with my feet.

—*Joan St. Once*

It's time to go on a diet when the man from Prudential offers you group insurance. Or when you take a shower and you have to let out the shower curtain. Or when you're standing next to your car and get a ticket for double parking.

—*Totie Fields*

My idea of exercise involves clipping a coupon and dialing the nearest pizza place.

—*Bill Jones*

I hate exercise. To me, getting up in the morning is a moving violation. The only exercise I get is pushing my luck, stretching the truth, and jumping to conclusions. I might carry a grudge.

—*Jason Chase*

On a diet? Go to the paint store—
you can get thinner there.

—*Bessie and Beulah*

I'm through exercising. For years I was doing everything I could to become "buff," only to find that I am evidently "buff-proof." I'm not working out now to get any better, but to keep from totally falling apart. Sad to say my washboard stomach has now turned into a Maytag.
—*Robert G. Lee*

It's pretty sad when a person has to lose weight to play Babe Ruth.
—*John Goodman*

I've been on a diet for two weeks and all I've lost is two weeks.
—*Totie Fields*

I get my exercise acting as a pallbearer to my friends who exercise.
—*Chauncey Depew*

Beefy George Reedy, one-time White House press secretary, was ordered by his doctor to the hospital to lose weight. When some White House aides sent him flowers, Reedy sent them this thank you note:

```
Thank you for the flowers.

They were delicious.

                    Reedy
```

—*Dear Wit*

Party Humor

The only way to combat criminals is by not voting for them.
—Dayton Allen

This chapter was just too easy to put together. Our government's primary goal seems to be supplying punch lines for comic monologues and jokes around the watercooler. Back as far as the 1920s, Will Rogers said, "I don't make jokes. I just watch the government and report the facts." Political punch lines are made of two things: what politicians *say* (Richard Nixon once declared, "I would have made a good Pope"), and what politicians *do* (Red Skelton said, "I don't pick on politicians. They ain't done nothin'").

There is something to tickle everybody in the pages that follow: jewels from Jay Leno, barbs from Bill Jones, and (my own) acronyms from Adam. You'll detect an underlying theme in many of the gags: Any government that gives you the freedom to make these kinds of cracks is still the best government around.

• • •

If God had wanted us to vote, he would have given us candidates.
—Jay Leno

CLINTON = Creating Legislation Increasing New
    Taxation On Nation
HILLARY = Healthcare Initiator Legislating Liberal
    Agenda Ruining You
GORE = Government Official Revering Environment
PEROT = Presidential Elf Reappearing On Television
DOLE = Dull Old People Lose Elections
BUCHANAN = Belligerent UltraConservative Harshly
    Attacking the National Administration Nowadays
RUSH = Republican's Uptight Stuck-up Host
—Adam Christing

The government spends so much money. I've heard that they recently put a box on the counter at the Treasury Department that says, "Need a billion? Take a billion! Got a billion? Leave a billion!"
—Bill Jones

Suppose you were an idiot, and suppose you were a member of Congress, but I repeat myself.
—Mark Twain

We have a presidential election coming up. And I think the big problem, of course, is that someone will win.
—Barry Crimmins

I don't belong to any organized political party—
I'm a Democrat.
—Will Rogers

Fun Raisers

Recently I performed at an animal rights barbecue.
—*Adam Christing*

Many politicians park in handicapped spaces because they are ethically impaired.
—*Bill Jones*

President Clinton was elected as the candidate of change. He wanted change, he promised change. Now he's got our change.
—*Steve Bridges*

The Right to Bear Arms refers to short sleeve shirts!
—*Bumper sticker*

You can always judge a man by what he eats, and therefore a country in which there is no free lunch is no longer a free country.
—*Arthur Baer*

C-SPAN's latest effort to attract more viewers looks like a winner. They're dubbing congressional coverage with a sitcom laugh track.
—*Bill Jones*

Our foreign dealings are an open book—
generally a checkbook.
—Will Rogers

Have you gotten your income tax papers yet? They've done away with all those silly questions now. There are only three questions on the form: (1) How much did you earn? (2) How much do you have left? (3) Send it in.

—Sandy Powell

An American is a person who yells for the government to balance the budget and borrows fifty dollars till payday.

—H. Alan Dunn

We're getting a lot of government these days, but we'd probably be worse off if we were getting as much as we're paying for.

—Olin Miller

Commenting on the Battle of Britain, Winston Churchill said, "Never have so many owed so much to so few. . . . If he were here to observe our Washington bureaucrats spending our tax money, he would say, "Never have so many done so little with so much. . . . "

—Bill Jones

Election Results

On Presidents' Day you stay home and you don't do anything. Sounds like *Vice* Presidents' Day!

—*Jay Leno*

Presidential candidate Adlai Stevenson was once addressing a very hostile audience that was booing and jeering his every attempt to speak. "Please, people," he implored, "I can hardly hear myself think!" At this, a thunderous voice from the back responded, "Mister, you ain't missin' much."

—*Bill Jones*

Do you know what's wrong with the world? England is in Palestine, Italy is in Ethiopia, Russia is in Spain, Germany is in Austria, Japan is in China—nobody stays at home!

—*Ed Wynn*

Liberals think you can reform an ax murderer. They don't want to kill anything. They want to change the Listerine labels: "*Rehabilitate* the germs that can cause bad breath."

—*Marc Price*

Money is so strange these days. Get a computer and take six months to pay for it. Get a new car and take six years to pay for it. Get a new government program, and in just sixty years your grandchildren will have it paid off.

—*Bill Jones*

The reason there are so few female politicians is that it is too much trouble to put makeup on two faces.

—*Maureen Murphy*

It is inexcusable for scientists to torture animals; let them make their experiments on journalists and politicians.

—*Henrik Ibsen*

My uncle invited me to a pro-life gun show.

—*Adam Christing*

Congressional terms should be ten to twenty with no possibility of parole.

—*Walt Handelsman*

Political ads are so scandalous, I always switch to a daytime talk show when they come on.

—*Bill Jones*

Crackin' Up the Congregation

Do you know what you get when you cross a Jehovah's Witness with an Atheist? Someone who knocks on your door for no apparent reason.
—Guy Owen

You're not supposed to laugh in church. Who made up that rule? God obviously has a great sense of humor; He made you and me, didn't He?

One of my best friends told me he became a Conservative Baptist. I said, "Isn't that redundant?" I can get away with this kind of joshing, because, as a churchgoer myself, he knows I'm laughing with him and not at him. These jokes and nutty observations razz a number of religions, and reflect my upbringing and my experiences performing for hundreds of denominations.

Maybe this will put some of the fun back into fundamentalism. Early Christians were known for their exhibitions of joy. The Rabbinical tradition is a rich source of humor. The Reformation was birthed in a battle of wits. By laughing together we can take ourselves less seriously and think more highly of God. *The Joyful Noiseletter,* and contemporary Christian comedian Robert G. Lee, along with other ministers of mirth, will bring some levity into your heart.

• • •

It often happens that I wake at night and begin to think about a serious problem and decide I must tell the Pope about it. Then I wake up completely and remember that I am the Pope.

—*Pope John XXIII*

You know it's going to be a boring service when the ushers ask for your espresso order as they hand you a bulletin.

—*Bill Jones*

My Karma ran over your Dogma.
—*Bumper sticker*

Some people say, "I go to church, so I am a Christian." But that's like saying if you go to McDonald's, you are a Quarter Pounder.

—*Adam Christing*

How odd
of God
To choose
the Jews.
—*Anonymous*

Not odd
of God.
Goyim
Annoy 'im.
—Leo Rosten

Christianity is filled with paradoxes. The Israelites expected the Messiah to be a great warrior and king. They *got* a carpenter. You generally don't expect the guy who's doing your kitchen cabinets to save the world.
—Robert G. Lee

I go to a huge church. It's so crowded they've started putting up those amusement park ropes outside the sanctuary to control the crowd between services. There's a sign at the end that says, "You are now forty-five minutes from the sermon."
—Robert G. Lee

Most people have some sort of religion; at least they know which church they're staying away from.
—John Erskine

He charged nothing for his preaching, and it was worth it, too.
—Mark Twain

I fear that one day I'll meet God, He'll sneeze, and I
won't know what to say.
—*Ronnie Shakes*

Here are some of the national headlines we may see
when Christ returns:

> *Time:* "He's Man of the Millenium!"
> *Parents:* "The Son of God—How to Raise an Over-
>   achiever"
> *Field & Stream:* "Fisher of Men Returns"
> *The National Enquirer:* "Christ Comes Back—And
>   He's Seen Elvis!"
> *Seventeen:* "Oh-mi-God!"
> *Self:* "God Comes Back for Me—Not You, Me!"
> *Atheist Monthly:* "Oops."
> —*Robert G. Lee*

There was a big flood in Louisiana. This guy is standing
in water up to his knees. They came by in a rowboat and
said, "Get in." He said, "Oh no, the Lord will take care of
me." A few minutes later he's up on the porch, the water's up to his waist. Another rowboat comes by, they say,
"Get in." He says, "Oh no, the Lord will take care of me."
Now he's on the roof. The water's up to his neck. A helicopter comes by. He says, "No, no, the Lord will take
care of me." Well, he drowned. He gets up to Heaven,
he meets the Lord, he says, "What happened?" The Lord
says, "I don't know what happened—I sent two row-
boats and a helicopter for you!"
—*Red Skelton*

They have a Dial-a-Prayer for atheists now. You can call up and it rings and rings but nobody answers.
—*Tommy Blaze*

A young girl once confessed to her priest that she thought she was guilty of the sin of pride. She said, "When I look in the mirror, I think I am beautiful." The priest said, "That's not a sin, that's a mistake."
—*Rev. James Whitcomb Brougher, Sr.*

Every week our preacher tells us to go out and "witness" to others. But nothing strikes more fear in my heart than having to share my faith with a complete stranger. It's gotten so bad I've enrolled in a Witness Relocation Program.
—*Robert G. Lee*

The Sunday school teacher was explaining to her students at a church in Hollywood what a wonderful book the Bible is. All of a sudden, one child raised his hand eagerly. "Teacher . . . have the movie rights been optioned yet?"
—*Bill Jones*

As a Hare Krishna, you might eventually reincarnate enough times to reach nirvana, but you have to spend so much time in airports to get there, who wants to bother?
—*Robert G. Lee*

St. Patrick's has a drive-in confessional.
You toot and tell.
—*Bessie and Beulah*

When the rector of a local parish was taken ill, the bishop of the diocese took his place one Sunday morning. At the end of the service, a group of church elders went over to thank him. "It was good of you, Bishop, to help us out today," one said. "A lesser man would have done, but we couldn't find one."
—*The Joyful Noiseletter*

What do you call a football player who becomes a born-again Christian? A two-point conversion.
—*Robert G. Lee*

My mother is Jewish, my father is Catholic. I was brought up Catholic, but with a Jewish mind. When I went to confession, I always brought a lawyer with me. "Bless me, Father, for I have sinned. . . . I think you know Mr. Cohen?"
—*Bill Maher*

Teaching Sunday school is for people who think they want children. But usually by the end of the hour, that urge has passed.
—*Robert G. Lee*

Some ministers would make good martyrs; they are so
dry they would burn well.
—*Charles Haddon Spurgeon*

Presbyterians are a rather conservative bunch. We're
like Methodists without the excitement. We never raise
our hands in church. We can't. We're afraid if we raise
them too high, God might call on us. In fact, we're so
conservative, Christ could come back tomorrow and
we'd form a committee to look into it.
—*Robert G. Lee*

Will Rogers came to talk to my congregation at Trem-
ont Temple one Sunday night. He jumped up, looked
around, and turning to the men on the platform, asked,
"Are these the deacons?"

I said, "Yes."

He replied, "I'm glad—I thought it was the Grand
Jury."
—*Rev. James Whitcomb Brougher, Sr.*

An Episcopal bishop was launching a campaign of
evangelism in his diocese. A sweet, elderly woman read
about the campaign, and when the bishop made his vis-
itation to her home, she kindly said to him, "Why,
Bishop, everybody that wants to be an Episcopalian already is one."
—*The Joyful Noiseletter*

I saw a bumper sticker that said, "God Is My Co-Pilot." I sped up to see who was driving. How good of a driver do you have to be for *God* to ride shotgun?

—*Brad Stine*

My wife and I went to a church retreat to ascertain our spiritual gifts. They asked if I had the gift of celibacy. I said I did, but I gave it back.

—*Robert G. Lee*

Tabloid headlines of biblical times:
"Moses Fasts 40 Days—Reveals New Super Diet"
"Prophet Daniel's Exciting Predictions for Next Millennium!"
"Elijah Kidnapped by Space Aliens!"

—*Phil Snyder, Hollywood Ministries*

Just as the prisoner was being strapped into the electric chair, the priest said, "Son, is there anything I can do for you?" The prisoner said, "Yeah, when they pull the switch, hold my hand."

—*Dick Gregory*

I think teaching Sunday school is impossible. The meek shall inherit the Earth. . . . The first shall be last. . . . The dead shall bury the dead. . . . You try teaching all that with finger puppets!

—*Robert G. Lee*

One Sunday, a minister appearing before his congregation with a bandage on his face, explained: "I was thinking about my sermon while shaving and cut my face." After delivering an unusually long sermon, the clergyman found this unsigned note in the collection plate: "Next time, why not think about your face and cut the sermon."

—Dear Wit

Catholic Church services are physically demanding. Standing, sitting, kneeling. Standing, sitting, kneeling. . . . Next week I think I'll try the low-impact mass.

—Scott Wood

Our church just built a new sanctuary. We couldn't afford it, but we did it anyway. Our campaign slogan was "Maybe God'll come back before we have to pay for it!"

—Robert G. Lee

Families Are Fun

Remember wearing hand me downs? I hated that. . . .
I have an older sister.
—Scott Wood

When my son was three years old, I was driving off to give a performance and he came darting out of the house. He was wearing only his Batman underwear and was crying intensely. I jumped out of my car and said, "What's wrong, Son?" He looked up at me with tears in his eyes and said, "Daddy . . . sob, sob, I didn't get to . . . sob, sob . . . hug you good-bye!" My heart nearly melted. He reminds me of this whenever he wants money for the ice-cream man.

Our families are to be treasured. But that doesn't mean we can't tease them, too. This last chapter of fun takes us back home, where you can relax, let your hair down—even pull it right off your head. Enjoy these zany comments about raising children, getting along with relatives, and parenting. And always remember the words of William Thackeray: "A good laugh is sunshine in the house."

• • •

If a man does not put away childish things, someone may drive over them coming into the garage.
—*The Humor Gazette*

When you're a parent, you're a prisoner of war. You can't go anywhere without paying someone to come and look after your kids. In the old days, baby-sitters were 50 cents an hour; they'd steam clean the carpet and detail your car. Now they've got their own union. They're charging Teamster wages out there. I couldn't afford it, so I had my mother come over. The sitters called her a scab and beat her up on the front lawn.
—*Robert G. Lee*

A family is a unit composed not only of children, but of men, women, an occasional animal, and the common cold.
—*Ogden Nash*

My parents sent my brother through law school. He graduated. Now he's suing them for wasting seven years of his life.
—*Mike Binder*

Before I got married I had six theories about bringing up children; now I have six children, and no theories.
—*Lord Rochester*

The fellow that owns his own home is always just coming out of a hardware store.
—*Kin Hubbard*

In high school my parents told me I ran with the wrong
crowd. I was a loner.
—*Jeff Shaw*

My brother just got his ear pierced. . . . Now he's got my
father's looks, and my mother's jewelry.
—*Scott Wood*

He was an angry man, Uncle Swanny. He had printed
on his grave: "What are you lookin' at?"
—*Margaret Smith*

My parents were very concerned about my moral edu-
cation. They continually applied the Board of Educa-
tion to the Seat of Knowledge.
—*Bill Jones*

Oh, give me a home where the buffalo roam—and I'll
show you a house full of dirt.
—*Marty Allen*

I've got a cousin who's thirty years old, unemployed,
and still lives at home. He's not the black sheep of the
family, he's the black hole of the family. His gravity center is so strong, no work can escape from him.
—*Robert G. Lee*

Happiness is having a large, loving, caring, close-knit family in another city.
—George Burns

My grandfather's a little forgetful, but he likes to give me advice. One day he took me aside and left me there.
—Ron Richards

Having children is like having a bowling alley installed in your brain.
—Martin Mull

Live that you wouldn't be ashamed to sell the family parrot to the town gossip.
—Will Rogers

For Further Fun

The show must go on.
—Greedy nightclub owner

Keep the laughs coming your way. Here is a listing of wholesome humor resources that may help you add a touch of fun to your next speech or presentation, bring some merriment to your home or office, teach you how to write or perform comedy yourself, and yes, even prolong your life with laughter! The major contributors to COMEDY COMES CLEAN and the following books and organizations can keep you grinning.

• Nick Arnette is the author of *The Encyclopedia of DUDE,* a clever 63-page collection of "dude-isms," i.e. Q: What do you call a dude from Switzerland? A: Yodela-heedude! To obtain a copy, write to P.O. Box 361180, Los Angeles, CA 90036, or call 1-800-456-1950. If you are interesting in booking Nick, refer to the last page of this book.

• *Head First: The Biography of Hope and the Healing Power of the Human Spirit* by Norman Cousins, 1990, Penguin U.S.A., 375 Hudson Street, New York, NY 10014. (1-800-253-2304.)

• *Holy Humor* is a tremendous collection of inspirational wit and cartoons compiled by Cal and Rose Samra, 1996, MasterMedia Limited, 17 East 89th Street, New York, NY 10128. (1-800-334-8232.)

- *The HUMOR Project, Inc.* publishes *Laughing Matters* magazine. For a free information packet on the positive power of humor, send a stamped ($1), self-addressed envelope to: The HUMOR Project, Inc., Dept CC, 110 Spring St., Saratoga Springs, NY 12866; call (518) 587-8770; or check out their web site at http://www.wizvax.net/humor/

- Bill Jones is the creator of *Brilliant Insights,* a funny fax service for speakers and writers which makes original customized comedy available to you on a moment's notice. For more information, call (714) 670-1929.

- *The Joyful Noiseletter,* the monthly newsletter of the Fellowship of Merry Christians, provides holy humor, clean anecdotes, upbeat stories, and cartoons about church life. Membership in the Fellowship includes a subscription to *The Joyful Noiseletter* and the F.M.C. catalog, which offers a variety of books, cassettes, and prints that focus on Christian joy and humor. Write to F.M.C., P.O. Box 895, Portage, MI 49081-0895, or call 1-800-877-2757.

- *Laugh-Makers* is a variety arts magazine for children and family audience entertainers. Write to P.O. Box 160, Syracuse, NY 13215, or call (315) 492-4523.

- Robert G. Lee can be seen every week on the new religious game show, *Inspiration Please,* on the Faith and Values network. For information on his audio and videotapes *Just Heaven Fun, The Laughs Are on Me,* and *Live at the Arrowhead Bowl,* write to P.O. Box 4152, West Hills, CA 91308-4152, or call 1-800-340-5004. For information about booking Robert for your group, turn to the last page of the book.

- The Nostalgia Archive restores classic films and comedy shorts from the 1920s, 1930s, and 1940s. For a free catalog of videos and other products, write to P.O. Box 790, Yorba Linda, CA 92686, or call 1-800-572-4624.

• *Phillips' Book of Great Thoughts & Funny Sayings,* by Bob Phillips, Tyndale House Publishers, Inc., Wheaton, Ill., 1993, is a handy compilation of witty quips and amusing observations. For more information about Bob Phillips's catalog of family fun books, write to Family Services, P.O. Box 9363, Fresca, CA 93702.

• *Gene Perret's ROUND TABLE* is a comedy newsletter published monthly for established and aspiring comedy writers and humorists. Write to 30941 W. Agoura Rd. #228, Westlake Village, CA 91361, or call (818) 865-7833.

• Brad Stine is an outrageous comic performer whose show is like being in the middle of a hurricane, tornado, and earthquake all at once. See the last page of this book for information about scheduling Brad for your next event.

• Scott Wood's comedy writing services can be obtained by writing to Scott Wood, c/o Lasting Impressions Comedy Productions, 558 E. Cypress St. #21, Covina, CA 91723, or calling (818) 966-2732. For free booking information, refer to the last page of this book.

About the Author

Adam Christing is the president of *Clean Comedians*, a Los Angeles–based entertainment company with comic entertainers and offices throughout the United States. He lives in Los Angeles with his wife and two children.